Reclaiming the "E" Word

Other books in the Lutheran Voices series

Reclaiming the "E" Word

Waking Up to Our Evangelical Identity

Kelly A. Fryer

Augsburg Fortress

Minneapolis

To Tana
"For freedom Christ has set us free."
—Galatians 5:1

RECLAIMING THE "E" WORD
Waking Up to Our Evangelical Identity

Scripture quotations, unless otherwise marked, are from the New Revised Standard Version Bible, copyright © 1989 by the Division of Christian Education of the National Council of Churches of Christ in the USA. Used by permission. All rights reserved.

Purchases of ten or more copies of this book are available at a discount from the publisher. For more information, contact the sales department at Augsburg Fortress, Publishers, 1-800-328-4648, or write to: Sales Director, Augsburg Fortress, Publishers, Box 1209, Minneapolis, MN 55440-1209.

Cover Design: Christy J. P. Barker
Cover photo © DAJ / Getty Images. Used by permission.

Library of Congress Cataloging-in-Publication Data
Fryer, Kelly A., 1961-
Reclaiming the "E" word : waking up to our evangelical identity / Kelly A. Fryer.
     p. cm.
ISBN 978-0-8066-8006-4 (alk. paper)
1. Evangelicalism. I. Title.
BR1640.F79 2008
270.8'3—dc22   2007041370

The paper used in this publication meets the minimum requirements of American National Standard for Information Sciences—Permanence of Paper for Printed Library Materials, ANSI Z329.48-1984.
Manufactured in the U.S.A.

12   11   10   09   3   4   5   6   7   8   9   10

Contents

Introduction

"Why are the churches that say they're welcoming to everybody always so small?"

Well, they are not always small, of course. Being "small," in and of itself, isn't exactly a problem. And just being "big" or even "growing" doesn't necessarily measure the things that I (maybe you and probably God) really care about. But those words were spoken out of frustration, concern, and love by my sixtysomething mom, a lifelong Roman Catholic who has grown increasingly impatient with the subtle and not so subtle sexism, homophobia, and hypocrisy—among other things—she believes she sees in too many churches, including her own. She had seen one of the "God Is Still Speaking" television ads, in which the United Church of Christ (UCC) creatively and courageously promises to be a church where everybody—no exceptions—is welcome and, for the first time in her life, got up on Sunday morning and didn't go to Mass. She attended a worship service at the local UCC congregation where she lives on the west coast of Florida instead. What she found was a very nice group of people in their seventies and eighties who, in the middle of Florida's immigration and housing boom, seemed resigned to presiding over the decline and inevitable death of their congregation.

"I just don't understand it," my mom said.

Well, I'm not sure I do, either. But I am quite sure that what I heard the day my mom phoned, discouraged and down, was a wake-up call.

What This Book Is About

If you are a member of a mainstream congregation in a mainline denomination, such as the Evangelical Lutheran Church in America, Episcopal Church, United Methodist Church, American Baptist Church, United Church of Christ, or Presbyterian Church (USA), it is likely that you are just as tired as my mom is of being held captive by the handful of people these days who seem to have hijacked the Christian faith and turned Jesus into a poker-faced, stick-in-the-mud, straighten-up-or-else-you're-going-to-hell, rule-making, line-drawing, fearmongering, gay-bashing, reason-defying, science-ignoring, flag-waving, saber-rattling, school-yard bully. If anybody dares to question this picture of Jesus or suggests that maybe we have gotten just a little off track, they are branded. Heretics. Pagans. Traitors. Antinomians (don't ask!). *Liberals.* Sometimes I wonder why we aren't rising up, in one single fluid we're-not-going-to-take-this-anymore movement, to shout with our loudest outside voices, "This is not the Jesus we know!"

But it's time. It's time for us to share the *really* good news about God's loving mission to save, heal, forgive, reconcile, and set free the whole creation and every single person in it. It's time for us to get out the word about Jesus, who sought after and welcomed those who had been cast aside, who shared his table with everyone, no questions asked and no exceptions made, whose radical, reckless love has torn down every wall that separates us from God and from each other. It's time for us to dare to deliver a message this world is dying to hear. It's time for us to reclaim the "E" word.

Historically, of course, mainline denominations have excelled at *showing* the love of Christ to their neighbors. We have built hospitals, schools, and orphanages. We have provided counseling, clothing, and care for the neediest in our communities. We have been the first to show up in times of disaster all across the globe, and we stay until the work is done, even after the TV crews turn off their cameras. Today Lutheran Services in America alone touches the lives of one in every fifty people who live in the United States and the Caribbean. Over the years, God has put our hands to good use. But our mouths, by and large, have been silent.

And in recent decades in particular, we seem to have been caught off guard by the ways in which our context has changed. Many of us seem to have convinced ourselves that, in an increasingly diverse world, our best option is to keep our faith to ourselves. Some of us have even begun to doubt that we have anything worth giving away.

Is it any wonder that our congregations keep getting smaller?

Let's take a deep breath and remind ourselves that the whole point of our lives as Christians, both individually and as a community of believers, is the other. It is our holy call, as followers of Jesus Christ, to share the good news of God with our neighbors in everything we do and say.

Imagine This

Imagine if evangelical didn't equal Christian Right.

Imagine if evangelical simply equaled Christian.

Imagine how the world would change if we began sharing the really good news with our neighbors without embarrassment and without hesitation. Imagine how different our communities would look if all those sleepy, centrist, and progressive mainstream congregations out there finally woke up and started telling the story of God's radical, unconditional, and transformational love with *evangelical* zeal. Imagine how the lives of our friends, family, coworkers, and schoolmates would change if we dared to let God shower them with love and hope and joy through the story that we have to tell. Imagine what it would look like for you to reclaim the "E" word for yourself. And what it would it look like for your faith community to reclaim it.

Imagine if the churches that say they're so welcoming were . . . really big!

I am not going to pretend otherwise: that is my hope, my prayer, and the number one reason I am writing this book.

My deepest desire is that those of you who share my frustration with the way our faith has been distorted in this culture over the past several decades will be inspired, motivated, and even equipped by something you read in these pages to reclaim the "E" word for yourself, for the sake of God's loving mission to save and set free the whole creation, and that your congregation will grow deep and wide as you do it.

The world needs what we have. For starters, I know firsthand that there is at least one woman in Florida who needs a new church home. There is no "snooze button" on this alarm. There is work to be done.

And the time is now.

1

A Wake-Up Call

Can you remember what you were doing the second weekend in November 2001?

I can.

For over a year, I had been scheduled to speak that weekend at a conference just outside of Washington, D.C. After the events of September 11, 2001, the conference organizers agreed they would not be frightened into changing their plans. (Easy for them to say because they were all *driving* to the conference!) Heeding the dire warnings about long lines at the airport, I arrived three hours early. Even so, I was the last one to the gate. Huffing and puffing, I made my way down the jet bridge and onto the plane, which was packed full, in spite of the fear that still gripped most of us. Pulling a little suitcase behind me and carrying both a guitar and a briefcase with my laptop in it, I made my way down the crowded aisle toward my seat. Naturally, it was the last one on the plane, backed right up against the bathroom.

As if I wasn't being intrusive (and annoying) enough, suddenly one of the flight attendants started walking toward me from the back of the plane—and talking to me. "You must be Kelly!" he said a little eerily and loudly enough to elicit glares from many of the other frazzled, frisked, and freaked-out passengers who suddenly realized the cause of their delay.

"A guitar, huh? Looks like you're going to be playing some music!" It felt, in the middle of that deadly quiet airplane, like he was shouting. "What kind do you play?"

"Umm . . . all kinds," I said, feeling my cheeks go red. He took some of my bags and helped me down the aisle.

"What are you going to D.C. for?" he continued.

"A conference," I answered quickly, trying as unobtrusively as I could to reach my seat.

"Sounds great! Are you playing your guitar at the conference?"

And so on.

This awkward banter continued all the way to the back of the plane, where he helped me stow my gear. After he moved away, I settled in for takeoff. I had just closed my eyes to rest as we backed away from the gate, when suddenly the "helpful" flight attendant reappeared.

"Kelly," he said softly, conspiratorial now, like the bit character in a bad spy movie or a fifth grade friend scheming something behind our teacher's back.

My eyes popped open to see him crouching down beside me.

"Yeeesss," I said suspiciously.

"See that guy sitting two seats in front of you on the other side of the aisle?"

Now, of course, he had my undivided, if completely baffled, attention.

"If he does anything suspicious, let me know."

Then he stood up and walked away.

I was dumbfounded. The first thing I thought was . . . (no, wait, my editor won't let me tell you the *first* thing I thought). The second thing I thought was that 9-11 must have made this poor young man go right off the deep end. But the third thing I thought was, *What if that guy does do something suspicious?*

I never took my eyes off the guy the whole way to D.C. In fact, as soon as the captain gave the "okay," I grabbed my laptop out of my bag because it was the heaviest thing I had to use as a weapon if need be.

Let's roll, I thought grimly.

Well, nothing did happen on that flight. We landed in D.C. and people piled off the plane, oblivious to the excitement going on (in my imagination, I mean) back by the bathroom. All the while we were deplaning, I was trying to decide whether to report the odd behavior of the flight attendant.

The man I had been "watching" was among the very last off the plane, of course. I was just a few feet behind him.

And so I got an eyeful as the huddle of D.C. police officers and FBI agents, who had been waiting for him on the Jetway, hauled him away in handcuffs.

Are you kidding me! I thought to myself, flabbergasted, as I shuffled numbly through the airport to find my shuttle. *You are totally kidding me, right? I mean, am I the best plan they've got?*

God Is Not Kidding

Well, I never did get an explanation for why that flight attendant chose me, of all people, to be his unofficial special agent that day. And I certainly hope the airlines have a better plan by now. However, the truth of the matter is—and now, finally, here's the point of the story—in a lot of ways, God's plan seems just as ridiculous!

We discover as we read the biblical story that, when it comes to God's loving mission to bless, save, reconcile, heal, and set free the whole world and every single person in it . . . we're it. You and I really are God's plan.

Strange as it may seem, God has always worked through ordinary people to get things done. As if setting the stage for all of history—and for our own personal stories—God told Sarah and Abraham, "I will bless you, and make your name great, *so that* you will be a blessing" (Gen. 12:2, emphasis added).

"Are you kidding me?" Sarah said to herself.

"Actually," God replied, "no, I'm not."

Jesus wasn't kidding either when right after he started telling everyone, "The time is fulfilled and the kingdom of God has come near," he gathered together the first guys he saw to help get that good news out to everybody (Mark 1:14-20).

"Follow me," he said to Simon and Andrew.

"For real?" they asked.

"For real," Jesus said.

To be a Christian is to be, at your very core, a participant in God's mission to love and bless the world. This loving mission comes *to* us, and it comes *through* us to others. In other words, it is our nature to be evangelical people. That is, we are people with good news to share. Really. That's what *evangelical* means.

The word *evangelical* has its roots in a Greek word that pops up all over the New Testament story of Jesus and his followers. The word *euangelion* means "good news." And I mean *really* good news—the kind that stops the presses and sets the blogosphere on fire. News so good it left a priest named Zechariah speechless (Luke 1:19-20) and got the angels singing (2:10). The kind of news that reaches even the deafest ears and gets the lame up dancing, news that could wake the dead (7:22). I'm talking about the news that Jesus himself came preaching (Matt. 4:23). This news came to each of us at some point in our lives. God's dream is for everyone to hear it. And God's plan is to make sure that happens through evangelical people like you and me.

Snap Out of It, People!

Now, I am aware that *Evangelical* has come to mean something very different over the past few decades, since it was first connected to a certain kind of "born-again" Christianity, to a network of conservative ministers and lobbyists who called themselves the new Christian Right in the late 1970s, and to the self-appointed Moral Majority that formed in 1979 for the sake of "restoring Judeo-Christian morality in American life."[1] In fact, it could be argued that the term has been distorted beyond recognition. That's why, not long ago, the editorial staff of a major U.S. newspaper provocatively asked, "Can the 'E-Word' be saved?"[2] And that's why some Christians, including many who have proudly considered themselves Evangelical, are saying probably not. Even the president of the Evangelical Theological Society, who is also a faculty member at Baylor University, says he has stopped using the word to describe himself. Instead, he says, "When I travel, I call myself a 'creedal Christian.'"[3]

The problem is that for most people, including many Christians, the "E" word has become associated with antiscience close-mindedness, biblical literalism, negativity, and mean-spiritedness. It's no wonder that, according to a recent Gallup survey sponsored by Baylor University, the term *evangelical* is losing favor even among the one in three Americans who belong to denominations considered Evangelical by theologians. Only 14 percent of Americans surveyed say this is one way they would describe themselves, and only 2.2 percent say this is the "best" term to use.[4]

John Buckeridge, the editor of the British magazine *Christianity*, believes "the tide has gone out" on the "E" word on both sides of the Atlantic. "To the unchurched and people of other faiths," he says, "evangelical is increasingly shorthand for: right-wing US politics, an arrogant loud mouth who refuses to listen to other people's opinions, men in grey suits who attempt to crowbar authorized version scripture verses into every situation, or 'happy-clappy' simpletons who gullibly swallow whatever their tub thumping minister tells them to believe."[5] Buckeridge and others are calling on "Evangelical" Christians to choose a new word to describe themselves. And frankly, under the circumstances, that might be a good idea.

But there are a whole bunch of other Christians out there, members of ordinary mainstream churches and historically mainline denominations, who really quite open to hearing other people's opinions; who have a deep commitment to ecumenical relationships with other Christians and even interfaith relationships with people of other religions; who know better than to think that Jesus belongs to any particular political party; who respect the Bible without turning it into an idol; who believe God has given us intellect and reason and imagination so that we can think for ourselves, explore distant horizons, and create new possibilities; who refuse to accept that one has to choose between science and faith; who really want our doors and our hearts to be open to everyone, even if we sometimes struggle over exactly what that looks like; who honor tradition but are willing to follow the Holy Spirit in new directions.

Unfortunately, we are painfully shy and lately have been woefully ineffective at communicating all this to others. In fact, about the only time anybody hears from us is when our denominational squabbles about sex spill out into the public square and a newspaper reporter catches us in the act. And so that's why we need to do just the opposite of what our (currently referred to as) "Evangelical" brothers and sisters are suggesting.

We need to be shaken out of our sleepy resignation and reawakened to our identity as people with good news to share. In other words, we need to reclaim the "E" word.

What Happened to Us, Anyway?

According to modern church historians, mainstream (also sometimes called "mainline" or "ecumenical") Christians, including most Lutherans, climbed into bed and pulled the covers over our heads sometime after about 1980.

And who could blame us? Since the end of World War II, the world around us has been changing faster than anyone except maybe Bill Gates could manage to keep up with. At first, from about 1946 to 1966, this meant changing a lot of diapers. This was the baby boom era. As Americans spilled out into new suburban communities looking for space to raise their growing families, churches sprang up across the landscape in unprecedented numbers. But those babies grew up—quickly. This meant, first of all, that all those brand-new church buildings, many of which had filled-to-capacity Sunday school wings, started emptying out as teens and twentysomethings went off to college or marched to war. But, second, as determined as their World War II–weary parents had been to build stable homes in quiet communities, those grown-up baby boomers—often encouraged and even led by pastors, theologians, and national church leaders—seemed determined to turn the whole world upside down. A lot of the world needed turning around, particularly from the perspective of marginalized, minority, multireligious, and multicultural groups.

It seems silly now to remember that, as a young girl with the best arm on my block, it took an act of Congress to open the local Little League to me. My dad coached my brother's team, and during practices, I was on the mound. Those kids knew that if they could hit my pitches, they could hit anybody's. If any of them could have fielded the ball, they would have had a great team! And it wouldn't have hurt to have the fastest pitcher in Hammond in their starting lineup. But I was sitting in the stands. Before Title IX was enacted in 1972, girls didn't just sit out when the boys played. They didn't play, period. And that reality was reflected in the lives of women in all kinds of ways.

It's hard to imagine, from where we are today, that elected officials in this nation ever dared to publicly argue for a whites-only water fountain, restaurant, school, neighborhood, or military. It's hard to imagine now the curbs of our city streets not accommodating wheelchairs or a public bathroom that a person with a disability can't use. It's ridiculous to think that there was a time when it was not only uncommon to see couples of mixed races holding hands; it was illegal. Although there is still much work to be done to ensure the fair treatment and equal rights of all God's children, the decades between 1950 and 1970 represent a heroic period in our nation's history and a heroic time even for many of our churches.

But it was also during this era, when people dared to question institutional authority and challenge the traditions responsible for propping up the powerful, that the seeds for our "post-everything" culture began to grow as if exposed to a sort of super-powered fertilizer. Nobody could have been prepared for the dramatic changes that would follow. Nobody was.

By the 1980s, as mainline Christians scratched their increasingly gray heads, wondering how to respond to this changing culture, a smaller and strident group of Christians grew confident that they had the answer. They were, they said, dismayed by the changes that had occurred over the past few decades. And they signaled their determination to reverse the trends. This radical group declared war on what they called the "secular humanism" that was responsible for a whole list of evils threatening the "traditional" family, including feminism, legalized abortion, the homosexual rights movement, church-state separation, declining morality, and girls in Little League (okay, I don't know if anyone ever actually said that!). Jerry Falwell, founder of the Moral Majority, told his congregants at Thomas Road Baptist Church in Lynchburg, Virginia, "The local church is an organized army equipped for battle, ready to charge the enemy. The Sunday School is the attacking squad. The church should be a disciplined, charging army. Christians, like slaves and soldiers, ask no questions."[6]

These radical Christians were as serious as the Pentagon brass in wartime about filling their pews. Professing a commitment to tradition and an allegiance to a "conservative" worldview, they nevertheless embraced and eagerly learned to leverage the power of new technologies and the media for the sake of communicating their message. And they were eager to flex their political muscle. These militant Christians formed alliances with unlikely partners, including conservatives across denominational and even interfaith lines, to elect favorite candidates. The antifamily enemy in their view meant anyone, including other Christians, who disagreed on social and political issues. In fact, this group took the credit for defeating the first "born-again" Christian president in U.S. history, Jimmy Carter, because they believed he was not supporting their "family values" agenda strongly enough. Suddenly, the dividing lines in American religion were no longer denominational or even theological. They were political.[7] And that meant they were ugly.

Facing the reality of an aging membership and underutilized buildings; challenged by an increasingly pluralistic, religiously diverse, postmodern culture; and terrified by the deeply politicized, mean-spirited Christian landscape—no one can blame us for wanting to dive under the covers. It's not hard to see why mainstream Christians have shrunk back from public life and chosen to keep the Good News to themselves, keeping it hidden even from their families, coworkers, and friends.

Well, brothers and sisters, it's time to shake off those covers and get up.

The world needs the good news we have to share! It is the same news Jesus brought with him. It goes something like this: "The kingdom of heaven has come near!" And in this kingdom, no one goes hungry, because people share what they have been given (Luke 9:10-17). In fact, the hungriest—and all those who would be left off most guest lists—have the best seats at the table (Mark 2:15-17). Prisoners are set free (Luke 4:18). Miracles happen as a result of the smallest acts (Matt. 13:31-32). The most unlikely people are instruments of kindness, love, and transformation (Luke 10:30-37). God's love knows no limits and recognizes no boundaries (Luke 2:32). There are no outcasts (Luke 15). This is the kingdom that Jesus brought in with him when he came. He announced this kingdom. He lived this kingdom. And he invited us to share the good news of this kingdom with everyone in all that we say and do.[8]

Stop the Pity Party

To be a Christian—right, left, center, upside down—is to have good news to share. To be a Christian, in other words, is to be evangelical. And it's time to stop letting our own self-pity and lack of confidence get in the way of that. Let's be honest. It's not like we can get the word out about Jesus from underneath our covers, still dressed in our pajamas, calling in sick because we feel sorry for ourselves. For the sake of the Good News and the world that needs to hear it—for our own sakes, for that matter—we just need to stop this.

Besides, exactly why are we feeling sorry for ourselves?

So we don't have as many people in the pews as we used to. There are still more mainstream, ecumenical Christians in the United States (an estimated forty-four million)[9]—when you add up all the Episcopalians, United Methodists, Evangelical Lutheran Church in America Lutherans, United Church of Christ, Presbyterians, American Baptists, and others who affiliate with each other through the National Council of Churches—than there are Evangelicals (an estimated forty million). If you are living in the Bible Belt, this might be hard to believe, but it's true. It is also the case that, over the past few decades, ecumenical membership has declined while membership in Evangelical congregations has increased. But there are a number of viable explanations for this besides "People don't like our theology" or "People don't like our politics" or "People just don't like *us*."[10]

One reason our buildings are emptier than they used to be is because a lot of the people who once filled them have died! Or retired to someplace sunny. We never should have built so many buildings in the first place, at least not the kind that we were unprepared to adapt for a new context. (It's hard to think about changing things in a building that cost a mint to build—and has Aunt Mildred's and Uncle Elmer's names plastered to the pews.) But, really, did we actually think the boom would last forever? My guess is that, for the most part, wherever you see empty Sunday school wings, you will also find public schools that, at some point over the past few decades, have been downsized or even abandoned and, at the very least, have had teachers who have worked hard (and probably with mixed results) to connect with a generation of kids who speak a whole new language. Mainstream churches and mainline denominations answered the call a half century ago, building facilities and an infrastructure to meet the needs of last century's baby boom. In some ways, this was our finest hour. There is no question that these churches have floundered trying to connect with new generations and growing ethnic populations, and their ties to the baby boom generation are at least partly to blame for that. In a number of ways, like a lot of organizations that grew along with the boomers, our struggles today are directly correlated to our previous successes. You might say we were too good for our own good. And it would be helpful to remember this.

There are plenty of signs that the religious Right is facing the same challenges we are. Published since 1900, the conservative *Moody Magazine* ceased publication in 2003 because Moody Bible Institute was in such a severe financial crunch. Similarly in 2003, for the first time in its twenty-six-year history, Focus on the Family had to eliminate one hundred jobs due to budget shortfalls.[11] One church historian observes that at the start of the new millennium, "even among thriving evangelicals . . . denominational loyalty was growing weaker, partly because Americans liked to experiment, shop around, and try different churches at different times in their lives," but also because one scandal after another has reminded "fundamentalists that even their leaders had feet of clay."[12] One Canadian television reporter who spent seven days in "God's Army"—that is, among Evangelicals in the U.S. Bible Belt—concluded that although he began his investigation thinking these radical Christians were out to impose their worldview on the rest of us, he now believes "they're more scared than scary."[13] The plight of our brothers and sisters on the radical Right should not give us reason to cheer. But it should help us get clear that we are not the only ones challenged by this complex and conflicted culture. The fact is, it's just hard figuring out how to be and do church in this new day.

With God's help we can do it. We can figure out how to get to know our new neighbors, how to communicate with new generations, how to make use of new forms of media, how to build new kinds of faith communities that are characterized more by online social networking than bricks and mortar. We can learn new languages, taste new foods, explore new cultures, and think of creative uses for all those old buildings. We can even begin to see what this increasingly postmodern culture—which values flattened hierarchies, authentic spirituality, purposeful living, and meaningful relationships—has to teach and offer us. I really believe we can find our way. But not if we insist on staying in bed, huddled under the blankets, pretending to be asleep.

Anyway, it is way past time to stop agonizing over the question, "Where did all our people go?" It's not helpful. Besides, some social scientists would remind us that the rumors about our decline and inevitable death are highly exaggerated. The truth is that, except for those few post–World War II years, when our bulging buildings made it seem as if we had the power to norm society, "mainline denominations have never really been that strong . . . [they] have always been somewhat distant and remote from the heartfelt religion of regular people, so this in nothing new. Mainline denominations have often wanted something more," more than just an emotional religious experience, more than individual salvation, more than personal morality. We have wanted to create a moral community[14] characterized, at its best, by mutual respect and responsibility, racial equality, and social justice for all. This vision did create a stir—and helped fuel the civil rights movement—in the 1950s and 1960s, but it has never fully captured the imagination of the majority of Americans.

At least, not yet.

Waking Up to Our Evangelical Identity

I'm committed to the renewal of mainstream Christianity because I believe the world needs what we have. That is why I took the opportunity, along with a team of researchers from the Evangelical Lutheran Church in America's Department for Research and Evaluation, to look under the hood of three of the ELCA's fastest-growing, large (attendance of one thousand or more at worship) congregations. I wanted to see what we could learn from congregations within a mainline denomination that have been built on the idea that to be a Christian is to be evangelical, that is, to speak the Good News to others, and have a proven ability to connect with others in their community in a dramatic way.

We chose our sample from a list of congregations compiled from trend reports and recommended to us by judicatory leaders (i.e., people in the bishop's office). Congregation A, which I will call "Alleluia Lutheran Church," had an average worship attendance of 1,245 at the time and, over the previous six years, had experienced a 59 percent growth rate. At Congregation B, which I will call "Blessing Others Lutheran Church," worship attendance was 3,500, growing at a rate of 53 percent over six years. Worship attendance at Congregation C, which I will call "Changed Lives Lutheran Church," was nearly 3,600, and they had grown by 175 percent over the same period. (In the past two years, this congregation has added another 1,000 people per Sunday, giving them a remarkable growth rate of 247 percent over an eight-year period.)

The reality is that most of the large, fast-growing congregations in the ELCA today are theologically "right of center." In many ways, they have more in common with their local Evangelical congregation than they do with others in their mainline denominational tribe. Most of them are in the Midwest too. But we really wanted to visit congregations that varied at least somewhat in worship style, theological perspective, moral/ethical positions, and geography. And so, to include a congregation from outside the Midwest in our sample, we added a fourth congregation to the study that did not meet the 1,000+ worship attendance criteria but is located on the West Coast, a region in which Lutheranism has had a hard time thriving. Congregation D is a theologically "centrist" congregation, which I will call "Making Disciples Lutheran Church." It had an average worship attendance of just over 400 at the time but a growth rate of 70 percent over the previous six years.

We worked with such a small sample so that we could do a "deep dive" into each one. Using proven qualitative research methods, we spent time "in the field" at each of these congregations. We made careful notes as we observed the congregation worshiping, engaging in educational opportunities, and participating in fellowship activities. We prepared a careful set of questions and recorded dozens of interviews with pastoral and lay staff, lay leadership, longtime members, and new members. These interviews were transcribed so they could, along with the notes we had made and the materials we collected, be searched for patterns and themes. Although we don't have a statistically reliable sample—it would have to be a little bigger for that—those of us on the research team were able to identify five things these congregations have in common, and we feel confident in our findings because these same themes emerged again and again in our interviews. And, although we aren't generalizing, we do believe that what we are saying about the churches we visited is true and may well be true of many growing churches.

Here is a summary of the five things we found these large, fast-growing congregations to have in common: (1) God is real to people, clergy and laity alike; (2) the Bible provides the framework for everything they do, think, say, decide, and dream; (3) they have a deep and real commitment to the priesthood of all believers; (4) the people, especially the leaders, are deeply pragmatic and willing to do whatever it takes to connect with new people; and (5) believing that God changes lives, everyone we talked to in these congregations expected something to *happen*!

Given the original list of congregations we had to choose from, I was not surprised to find those in our sample exhibiting some characteristics stereotypical of "Evangelical" congregations in the United States that made me a little uncomfortable. For example, the "transformations" that were described by people and expected by the congregational leadership were overwhelmingly individualistic (i.e., people "getting their lives together"), rather than the kind of Matthew 25 transformation that leads people to give themselves away for the sake of the poor, the outcasts, the hurting, and the hungry. Furthermore, their preexisting sympathy to a politically conservative "family values" agenda tended to both influence and be reinforced by a literalistic interpretation of Scripture in an all too familiar hermeneutical circle.

I walked away from this project more interested in what we can learn from these places than in trying to fix or even critique what I think they might have wrong, and I am deeply grateful to them for allowing us to take a peek under the hood.

In fact, based on what I learned from studying these congregations, what I know from working with thousands of church leaders and congregations across the United States and Canada over the past ten years, what I hear when I listen to God's voice through the biblical story, and what I know of the wisdom that has been passed on to us by Christians across the centuries, I believe that, if we are serious about reclaiming the "E" word in mainstream congregations and across mainline denominations, it will mean being willing to:

- Wake up to the real deal.
- Wake up to a vital word.
- Wake up to a purposeful life.
- Wake up to our common call.
- Wake up to transformational power.

God has given us a remarkable story and really good news to tell. The kingdom of heaven has come near! Over the past few decades, this hasn't always sounded like good news from those who have been speaking for the radical Christian Right. And the rest of us, for all kinds of reasons, have been asleep on the job.

It's time to wake up and get to work. After all, weird or not, we really are God's best plan.

Wrestling with the Word

1. What is your favorite Bible story? Tell it or read it out loud. In what way is this story good news for you and your life?

2. Nobody has ever done a better job of telling the good news of Jesus than the apostle, Paul. His life is also an illustration of how God's loving mission comes *to* us and *through* us to others. Read Paul's story in Acts 9:1-19. God's love comes to Paul through Ananias. How—and through whom—has God's love come to you, lately? Tell somebody about that. God also said that Paul

would be an instrument through whom God's name would be brought to "Gentiles and kings and before the people of Israel" (v. 15). How has God's love come through you to someone else lately? Tell somebody about that too.

Thinking Things Through

1. In what ways do you think your congregation is asleep? How, why, and when did this happen? What will it take to wake it up? What do you think you can do to help make that happen?

2. How would you describe the good news to someone who hasn't heard it before? What difference has the good news made in your life? How eagerly do you share this story with others? If the answer is "not very," why not? What needs to change in your heart or mind for you to reclaim the "E" word in your own life?

3. Where is the most unusual or surprising place you have learned something helpful? What do you think about the idea that we might have something to learn from "large, fast-growing congregations" that, theologically, lean a little right of center? What prejudices or hurts, if any, do you need to set aside to learn something from the next chapters?

Talking It Over

Dear God, we give you thanks for the good news and for your call to share it with everyone. Clear away whatever has been preventing us from doing that and fill us up with evangelical zeal with this purpose. Wake us up! In the name of Jesus, amen.

2

Waking Up to the Real Deal

A former student, from my days as a seminary teacher, now delights in teaching me a thing or two from his perspective as, what is called "in the business," a "mission developer." In other words, he is planting a brand-new faith community. We get together once in a while for lunch and stay connected via e-mail. He gets to bounce ideas off of me, dazzling me with his creativity and his passion for doing church in new ways, and I get to remind him about all the things he has forgotten from my classes. I'm smiling here. Our conversations feed me.

This is from our last energetic exchange, in a conversation about what the good news is and about our call as Christians to share it: "People want to know that God is real," he just about shouted at me across the Web, "and that God is involved in this world and in their lives. When the s#*! hits the fan, they hope and pray that what they have said they believe is true."

A Little Doctrine Goes a Long Way

God has never *not* been real to me. My family is Roman Catholic, remember? When I was a child, God was so real that I thought we had captured him (or, at least, a little piece of him) and put him in that gold-trimmed box on the altar. (And God was a "him" to me then.) That's what all the genuflecting was about when we went into church, I was told, even when Mass wasn't going on. Jesus Christ, the second person of the holy Trinity, the Lord of lords and the King of kings, God's own Son, was really present in that Host. And, when you were in his presence, there was no messing around.

This feeling of being in the "real presence" of God, I thought then, lessened the farther away I got from the building. And I wasn't too crazy about that because, frankly, as a kid, I could have used a little more holy help than I felt like I was getting. But there was no question in my mind that God was real. And God was everywhere. In fact, if God couldn't be there for some reason, you had a guardian angel just in case. And you always had the saints! There were always at least a couple of them around to help you when you got lost or your friends were picking on you or you had a long trip to take or you were scared of the dark.

Even during those horrible college years when I was so angry at God that I invested myself in convincing everybody around me that God wasn't real (sorry, guys), I never doubted the presence of God. Most of what I did in those years was meant to tick God off. And you don't bother ticking off somebody you think isn't real, doesn't matter, or isn't around to see it.

To be honest, even though God and I made up after those rocky years, we still have a sort of strained relationship. I am more thankful than I can say for all the blessings God has poured out upon my life. "Praise God from whom all blessings flow!" was the first lullaby I sang to my newborn daughter twenty-some years ago. I had no doubt that the miracle I held in my arms that first night of her life was straight from God. God has continued to bless me in all kinds of ways, filling my life with surprising discoveries, new opportunities, and undeserved "do-overs." But, dang it all, God keeps asking me to do things I don't want to do. My mother says I have always had a problem with authority. And maybe that's part of why God and I struggle so much. But the bottom line is that no matter what is happening in my life, good or bad, I have always known that God is right here in the midst of it all.

As I have become a bit more theologically sophisticated, I have come to understand that the "experience" of God's presence isn't reliable enough to build one's faith on. In fact, assigning too much value to personal experience when it comes to God can be downright dangerous.

What happens, for example, when you *feel* far away from God? Do you actually *believe* God is far away? You might unless you have been taught that God's word is reliable and that in the written word of God, we have been given a promise that "neither death, nor life, nor angels, nor rulers, nor things present, nor things to come, nor powers, nor height, nor depth, nor anything else in all creation, will be able to separate us from the love of God in Christ Jesus our Lord" (Rom. 8:38).

According to her letters, which have recently been released for the first time, this was exactly the situation Mother Teresa faced for most of the last fifty years of her life and ministry. Her personal spiritual life appears to have been an "arid landscape." She describes *feeling* agonizingly far away from God's presence, power, and love. Yet she gave herself away in Christ's name, in service to people in the most desolate places on earth. In fact, some who have been working toward her canonization as a saint within the Roman Catholic Church are arguing that her ability to minister even as she faced this ongoing spiritual emptiness is the greatest miracle of all. Perhaps it is. It is just as much, I think, a sign that true faith cannot be built on our *experience* of God alone.[1]

Could you, for example, come to believe that God's free gift of grace through faith in Jesus Christ is actually dependent on your ability to chalk up enough good works because your life experience tells you that you are not worthy enough to get it any other way? You might unless you have a solid foundation built on this central, doctrinal truth that we are "justified by [God's] grace as a gift, through the redemption that is in Christ Jesus" (Rom. 3:23).

If all you have is your experience of God, you might, in fact, lose your way. And throughout the history of the church, we have seen that happen. Doctrine matters. Doctrine represents the collective wisdom of the two thousand years' worth of discussion, debate, and discernment that have gone on before us, carried out by smart and faithful women and men throughout the history of the church. A really healthy faith knows that history and knows how to use it. A healthy faith is at least partly a "head" thing.

But a little doctrine goes a long way.

It All Starts Here

Knowing "the faith" and knowing *God* are two very different things. Both are important. But Protestantism has always struggled to keep them in balance. As far back as 1675, just about 150 years after the Reformer Martin Luther and friends got the party going, an Evangelical (which is what Lutherans were called in Germany back then and still are today) pastor named Philipp Jakob Spener was complaining that the church was sucking the life out of people. "It is by no means enough," he said, "to have knowledge of the Christian faith." But, he said, too many church leaders are only interested in "making people Lutheran and do not deem it important that with this profession such people become genuine Christians to the very core. They therefore regard true confession of faith as merely a means of strengthening their own ecclesiastical party and not as an entrance upon a life of zealous future service of God."[2] Spener's harsh critique of the church in his day, that basically all the church cared about was getting more people in the pews, didn't go over well, as you can imagine. Even today there are a lot of Christians in the Lutheran tribe who aren't so fond of the guy. He scares them. And maybe he should. But his point is well taken.

Just knowing *about* God isn't enough. It never was.

In the biblical story, God didn't send people *ideas*. God sent *people*. At first, God sent prophets and priests and kings. God sent ordinary people like Sarah and her old husband, Abraham, and Moses and his sister, Miriam. And finally, at just the right time, God sent Jesus. In fact, Jesus *was* God, coming to people in the flesh. Through Jesus, God was as real to people as real can be. John and James, Martha and Mary, the woman at the well, the man born blind—all of them experienced the Good News firsthand. And that is what made all the difference. Jesus forgave them, healed them, taught them, and opened their eyes and helped them see. Jesus raised them from the dead. Jesus called them, as undeserving and unlikely as they were, to come follow him. And that was the Good News, the amazing story they had to tell others. In fact, they couldn't not tell this story, even when they were threatened with prison and bodily harm.

Peter and John were so good at telling their story that one day they got themselves arrested. The crowds were too big. The people were too excited. And, as a result, the "priests, the captain of the temple, and the Sadducees came to them, much annoyed" (Acts 4:2). These guys were especially upset because Peter and John were telling the story about how they had seen Jesus after he had been raised from the dead. I imagine it sounded something like the following.

Breathless with excitement, having a hard time getting all his words out quickly enough, Peter said to the gathered crowd, "And then . . . and then . . . the women came running back from the tombs. They had gone there to care for the body, of course. But they said to us, 'There is no body!' They said, 'There were *angels* at the tomb, instead!' And the angels told them that Jesus had been raised from the dead! They said they ran back to tell us as quickly as their feet could carry them. They don't even know what happened to all the oils and spices they were carrying. *Who needs these?* they must have thought, casting them to the side of the road like that old blind man did with his beggar's cup after Jesus spit into the clay and healed him. Remember that day, John? We've had quite an adventure, haven't we, John?

"Okay," Peter said, remembering the listening crowd, "where was I? Oh, right! So the women get back and tell us this whole crazy story. And, get this: no one believes them! Nobody except me, that is! I took off running, and my name isn't Peter the Rock if those women weren't telling the truth. There was nothing inside that tomb except the cloth we wrapped Jesus in.

"I am not making this up!

"That same day, two of our buddies said they saw Jesus on the road to Emmaus. They even ate dinner with him! He showed up a bunch more times after that too. I saw him. And John here saw him as well. Didn't you, John?

"Well, speak up, John! Tell them. . . ."

Peter and John didn't give lectures to people about all of the great ideas they had about God. Instead, they told people a story. They told the only story they had to tell. They told about the resurrection power they had seen with their very own eyes. For that they were thrown in jail. The authorities were afraid of making the enthralled crowds too angry, and so after a big conference, they decided just to scare the two disciples a little. We are ordering you, the priests said, "not to speak or teach at all in the name of Jesus. But Peter and John answered them, 'Whether it is right in God's sight to listen to you rather than to God, you must judge; for we cannot keep from speaking about what we have seen and heard'" (Acts 4:18-20).

In these disciples we see what the evangelical life looks like. They couldn't be stopped from telling about what they had seen and heard. They had a remarkable story to tell about the God who had come to them in Jesus Christ, a God who loves and forgives and heals, and who calls even the most unusual and unexpected people to be his witnesses.

One contemporary Lutheran theologian puts it plainly: "In the end, all evangelical ministry boils down to the reality of Jesus coming to people."[3] In other words, waking up to our evangelical identity happens as God becomes real to us.

An Unexpected Visit

In many mainstream congregations today, reclaiming the "E" word will have to begin with waking up to God's real presence among us. I don't think I'm exaggerating when I say this could be a real problem. It isn't that we don't "believe" in God. It's just that, often, we act like we don't believe God is really here.

A couple of years ago I met an unusual woman at a church conference. The fact that she was a woman isn't what made her unusual; there are a lot of women at church conferences. Nor was she unusual because of her age; she was probably fifty-five, the age of a lot of mainline church people these days. What made her unusual was that she looked and sounded as if she was on fire for God. She was so eager to be a part of God's dream to love and bless and save the whole world that she was contagious—or scary, depending on how long it has been since you last experienced the real presence of God in your own life. Anyway, she told me that she was back living in her hometown after about twenty-five years away. Her parents were needing a little extra help, so she had packed up her life and bought a house next door to them. This meant joining the same congregation she had grown up in. And, God help them, it *was* the same. In almost every way.

She rapped her knuckles on the table we were sitting at. "It was deader 'n this here table," she said.

Did I tell you she was from Texas?

After a little agitating, she got folks in her church to agree to form a "strategic planning committee." They put her in charge of it. At her first meeting, she got them doing Bible study together. Some of the guys even prayed out loud when she asked them to, although they weren't necessarily very happy about it. And then they brainstormed. They made a long, long list of things their congregation could do in their community to connect with people in a meaningful way, to live out God's love for everybody.

They sat looking at the list for a while. And then one of the guys said what everybody else around the table was probably thinking.

"Who's gonna do all this?" he asked.

"God," she answered. And she believed it.

But she could tell by their faces they didn't. And she knew nothing was going to happen in that little congregation until they did—until they believed that God is *real.*

A few weeks later, she happened to be walking through the church when the decorating committee was getting the place decked out for Christmas. The tree (artificial, at least twenty years old, given by some old saint long dead but living on in that dusty old tree) was sitting cockeyed in the stand, waiting for some attention, on the right side of the altar.

"You know," the contagious, scary lady said, "I think it'd look better over on the left side."

"But it's always on the right side," she was told.

"Why?" she asked.

"It's been on the right side for at least thirty-eight years."

"But why?" she asked again, probably thinking, *Wow, that tree doesn't look a day over twenty.*

No reason.

None.

So she marched right up to the front of the church, picked up that old tree, and moved it to the left side of the altar. Nobody moved. Nobody said anything. They were, I think, waiting for the thunderclap of God's wrath to sound the end of days. After a long silence, somebody finally started breathing again.

"Hey," said one of the decorators, "that looks pretty good."

She got him to help her move it the last few inches. They hung lights on it together.

On Christmas Eve that year, for the first time in recorded history (longer even than thirty-eight years), it snowed in that little Texas town—twelve inches. The snowstorm, I'm told, made national news.

Now this woman didn't believe for a second that moving that old tree and their record snowstorm were connected. But that didn't prevent other people in the congregation from making the connection. And she didn't stop them. How else could you explain the blanket of white that had descended upon them from on high?

For the first time in a long time, people in that congregation had a light in their eyes. People were walking around feeling as if they had seen a miracle happen, feeling as if they had been part of a miracle. Suddenly they knew how the people of Nain (Luke 7:11-17) must have felt the day their funeral was interrupted by a strange man named Jesus who, as he was passing through their little town, said, "I hope you can use all those little ham sandwiches for something besides a funeral luncheon, because this boy is not exactly dead anymore!" They believed they had been visited by God.

And for the first time in at least, well, thirty-eight years, they began to think that, just maybe, new things were possible.

A Telling Difference

It shouldn't be that hard to get our heads around the idea that people need to experience the real presence of God. This is the whole point of "the word, sacraments, and Christian community,"[4] right? Since the Protestant Reformation more than five hundred years ago, we have been teaching that Jesus comes to us when the word is spoken in a sermon, in the promise of forgiveness that is declared during our Sunday morning worship service, or even by a friend who tells us that God loves us, forgives us, and wants to bless us. Jesus comes to us in a way that we can actually feel, when the water of baptism splashes over us or the wine of Holy Communion is poured. Jesus comes to us through the gathered people, our brothers and sisters in faith, who witness to us about their faith and encourage us to answer Christ's call. In fact, one of the biggest ideas of the Reformation—that we are saved by grace through faith in Jesus Christ—depends on Jesus coming to us. God always comes down![5] There is, we teach, absolutely nothing we could ever do to be worthy enough to make our way to God. God, through Christ, always comes to us. For real.[6]

But in too many of our congregations, the sacraments have become hollow rituals, the word falls silent after the sermon is over, and everybody thinks it's the pastor's "job" to talk to and speak for God (after she finishes doing all the hospital visits and typing up the bulletin, of course). Too many people in too many of our congregations feel that God hasn't visited them in a very long time. It is remarkably difficult to get people to try new things, to believe that things can be different, to trust God enough to risk moving in new directions. Way too few of us are contagious and scary. And when was the last time you met somebody so full of good news, so eager to tell his story, that he couldn't be stopped from sharing it with everyone he met? Why when you turn to the guy sitting next to you in the pew or at the church council table and ask him what God has been up to in his life lately, he looks at you as if you have lost your mind? Why has the light gone out of our eyes?

Well, if this describes the situation in many mainline congregations today, we found a telling difference in the congregations we studied. Again and again in our interviews, people explained to us that one of the main reasons they keep coming back is the sense that God is alive and active there. In fact, across the board, people didn't just talk about God. They talked about God as if God were literally in the room. Indeed, they believe God is in the room! But—and here's the news that's going to be hard to hear—they said this is different from anything they have experienced anywhere else before.

The president of Changed Lives Lutheran Church says he has moved around quite a bit and been a member of many Lutheran churches around the country. What really stands out for him in this faith community is that it helps people build a relationship with Christ. It is "exceptional," he says. People are encouraged to develop a "true relationship" with God instead of just "going through the motions." Similarly, at Disciple Making Lutheran Church, every single layperson I spoke with could tell me that at the heart of the teaching at this congregation is the truth that "we are saved by grace." But most of them also had stories about how God's grace had been made real to them through the ministry of this congregation.

Alice[7] is the vice president of Alleluia Lutheran Church. She also joined this new congregation after a relocation from another town. Although she had been raised in a churchgoing Methodist family, she admitted that she had been "a flatliner in spiritual growth for twenty years." The congregation she belongs to now, she says, encourages her to be more than "just" a believer. She is "developing a relationship with Jesus Christ."

While only two or three of all the people we spoke to complained directly about their experiences in previous churches, it was clear that they had found something different in this new faith community. Across the board, in one way or another, this is what we heard them say: God is real for them now in a way that God had never been real for them before, even if they had been members of another church all their lives. You might say Jesus has become a real *person* to them, someone with whom it is possible to be in relationship.

"Why do you think people come here?" we asked one of the pastors at Blessed to Be a Blessing Lutheran Church. His response was simple: "Because it's real." In this congregation people "are learning about a God who loves them and can change lives."

Now, I don't really believe that God is doing more in these congregations than anywhere else, do you? After all, Jesus is showing up for people wherever the word is proclaimed, the sacraments are received, and the Christian community is gathered. That's what we teach, right? But, for some reason, people in the congregations we studied are able to see it; and having seen it, they can't stop talking about it.

Furthermore, one of the really striking things about the conversations we had with people in these congregations is that they didn't just talk about what God was up to in their congregations. They talked about what God was up to in their everyday lives. They talked about

God as if God was on the loose in the world and up to something they wanted to be a part of.

For example, one member of Changed Lives Lutheran Church, who had joined the congregation after relocating due to a job transfer, said it might seem like his job is the reason he came to town. But he believes God sent him there for another reason. "God is doing something [in the congregation and in this town]," he said. And he believes God wants him to be a part of it.

This man believes that God is real and at work in his town, in his work, and in his everyday life. God isn't stuck in a box in these congregations. You don't get farther away from God the farther away from the building you go! People in these congregations talked with ease about what God was up to in their everyday lives, not just their "church" lives.

What's Going on Here?

It is important to note that we did not prompt people to talk about God during our interviews. In other words, we didn't ask them, "So, what has God been up to in this congregation [or your life or your community] lately?" Rather, we asked open-ended questions, such as, "What attracted you to this congregation?" and "What do you like about this congregation?" and "What don't you like about this congregation?" People responded in a variety of ways, as you can imagine, but again and again they testified to the presence and the reality of God at work in their midst and in their everyday lives.

I can't explain why people in these congregations are so able to sense God's presence or so willing to talk about what God is up to. But I did observe something during my visits that might give us a clue: The leaders and pastors of these congregations work hard at helping people see God in action.

First of all, the leaders themselves easily and often talk about what God is doing in and through the congregation. This may help set a tone and give people an example to follow. It could be that the willingness of leaders to say what they hear God saying and see God doing gives others courage to do the same. For example, one of the assistant pastors who helped lead one of the several worship services at Changed Lives Lutheran Church the weekend we visited began by saying to the 1,400-plus people who had gathered, "It's no accident that you're here. We've been praying for you. We believe God has brought you here and wants to touch your life. You are among friends."

"We believe God has brought you here," she said. In other words, "We believe God is doing stuff and wants you to be doing stuff too."

This is language I don't hear very often in most mainline congregations. Not even from pastors. And I think this matters. It's one thing for a pastor—or for any of us—to share our opinions, even courageous and creative ones, such as:

"We should start a homeless shelter."

"People are so lonely in our neighborhoods. We each should sponsor a block party and give people a chance to get to know one another. Who knows, maybe we'll make some new friends too. And if they seem interested, we could invite them to worship with us."

"We should just sell this big old building and use the money to plant a bunch of experimental ministries in different places around the city to try and connect with new people in a new way."

Good ideas. But when developed and presented this way, they are just *our* ideas. And I'm convinced one of the reasons it's so hard to get things done in most congregations is that everyone has a different one! Imagine how different it would be if people were not only listening for God's voice speaking to them through the Holy Spirit, but they were talking about listening for God's voice speaking to them through the Holy Spirit. Imagine what it would be like if, in our congregations, we were listening for God's voice together. Here's what it could sound like:

"You know, I really believe God is telling us that we should start a homeless shelter. What are you hearing?"

"I know this might sound wacky, but I think I'm hearing God say that we should sell this big old building, and. . . . What are you hearing?"

God is speaking to us, of course, through the Holy Spirit. Jesus promised that would be the case (Acts 1:8). God is leading us, guiding, us, nudging us, challenging us, planting dreams in our hearts, giving us courage to take risks for the sake of our neighbors, and gifting us with everything we need to be witnesses to the kingdom. God is among us as we work together to be and do church in the places where we have been planted.

In the congregations we studied, the leaders were willing to claim that. But they were also very intentional about helping others see it too. For example, on Sunday mornings during the season we visited Blessed to Be a Blessing Lutheran Church, the pastors were preaching a sermon series called "A Faith That Works," which explored what Jesus has to say about everyday things, including worry, money, divorce, and judging others. Each week a "Kingdom Moments" video was shown in which ordinary members of the congregation would tell about how God had been at work in their lives during times of hope, hardship, grief, and brokenness.

At Alleluia Lutheran Church, Alice said her relationship with Jesus Christ is developing and she wants to help others experience the same thing. That's why she decided to participate in an adult study program at the church called "Experience in God." Through this study, Alice explained, participants learned a process of self-exploration, a way to recognize God at work, a way to become engaged in the word, and a way to join God's work in the world.

God is real to Alice inside the four walls of her congregation where she hears the word and shares Christ's Supper and is nourished by her relationships with others in the community of faith. But she doesn't think for a moment that God's presence can be boxed in by buildings. Rather, because of the way Jesus has come to her within her congregation, he is real to her everywhere she goes.

The Real Deal

"People want to know God is real," my student-teacher tells me. And I'm sure that's right. In fact, I'm quite sure this is one of the reasons our sample congregations are connecting so successfully with people. They are meeting that need. But I would add this: God really is real. As important as our ideas about God might be, God did not send an idea two thousand years ago. In Jesus, God came to people and gave those first Christians something to talk about. That was the story Peter and Paul, Lydia and Priscilla, and the women who discovered the empty tomb all had to tell. And God, through the power of the Holy Spirit, comes to us still. This is where our evangelical identity begins. Reclaiming the "E" word means waking up to the real deal and being open to the experience of God's presence in our lives, in our congregations, and in our world. But I don't believe this will just happen by itself. We need to be diligent about paying attention to God's presence in our midst, especially in those places where God's word has been shrunk to the size of a sermon or people have grown numb to it even at the Lord's Table. We need to be intentional about learning to listen for God's voice (rather than our own ideas and opinions) in our congregations but also, and maybe especially, in our seminaries and regional and churchwide offices. Our leaders need to be setting the tone. And, maybe most important, those of us who spend a lot of time "inside" these walls need to remember that God is also on the loose "out there." The God who came to us in Jesus two thousand years ago comes to us today in the middle of our everydays, not only wherever we gather, but also wherever we go. See that, and you won't be able to stop talking about it.

Wrestling with the Word

1. In the "Bible wars" we see happening in our culture today, sometimes it is easy to forget that the Bible is just one way that God speaks to us. The Gospel writer John reminds us that God's word is alive. The word of God "became flesh and lived among us" (1:14). The word of God is Jesus Christ. Read the first chapter of John's Gospel. What do you hear God saying to you through these words?

2. Reflecting on this first chapter of John, tell someone about where have you experienced God "living" lately—in your family, your community, your congregation, your workplace? Where—in

whose heart or home—do you think God wants to be dwelling? What do you hear God calling you to do about that?

Thinking Things Through

1. Does it seem as if your congregation is being guided by the Holy Spirit as you are making decisions together, or are you swayed more by the opinions and ideas of the most influential, powerful, or vocal members? What makes you say that?

2. God doesn't send ideas; God sends people! Through whom has God come to you recently? What was the good news he or she had to share? What difference did it make for you?

3. Why do you think some Christians act as if God never leaves the building? What would happen if we got our heads wrapped around the idea that God is on the loose in our world? What would be different for you at home, at work, or at school? What would be different about the way you vote and invest your money?

Talking It Over

Dear God, we are so thankful for all of the ways that you are really present for us—in our lives, in our congregations, and in our communities. Forgive us when we fail to recognize that and act as if we are on our own. Help us to be more intentional about being on the lookout for you everywhere we go. Open our eyes to see you and our ears to hear you. Give us great stories to tell! We pray in Jesus' name. Amen.

3

Waking Up to a Vital Word

Back in the good old days when my son was shorter than me and not yet tall enough to lean with his chin on the top of my head, we would play a game he named "Stump the Chump." Here's how it would go:

"Matthew 5!" he would shout at me.

And I would say, "Umm, let me see. . . . I think that's probably the Sermon on the Mount."

"Isaiah 2!" he would fire back.

"That's where God is telling the prophet what he's supposed to do. It's part of the vision God gave him."

"Luke 32!"

"There isn't a Luke 32."

"Okay, Luke 22!"

"Hmm, that's toward the back of the book. I'm thinking that's about where Jesus gets arrested and killed."

I know, pastor's families are weird. But my boy was very impressed by my performance in this little game. Little did he know that, although I never flat out fibbed, I did take some pretty wild guesses. I'm glad he never checked my answers!

Welcome to the Chump Club

Stump the Chump is actually a pretty good name for a theologian's game. Martin Luther said the most important characteristic of a theologian is humility. And it is this idea that lies at the heart of what Lutherans call "a theology of the cross." The point is that basically we are all chumps when it comes to trying to figure out what God is up to.

God doesn't do anything the way we would expect. For example, in the Bible, God always uses the most unqualified people who can be found to do the most important things. It is as if God looks out over the planet for all the people who are the smartest, most talented, most powerful, and most obvious choices and says, "Umm . . . no."

There are few better examples of this than the story of Gideon and the Midianites (Judg. 7:15-25). Gideon had an army thirty thousand strong, the ablest and fiercest men of Israel. And he needed every one of them because they were facing a Midianite army so enormous it was "as thick as locusts," at least one hundred twenty thousand troops. Even their camels were "without number, countless as the sand of the seashore" (v. 12). But before the battle, the Lord spoke to Gideon and told him to send half of his men home.

With a God like that, you may be wondering, *who needs enemies?*

God explained it this way to Gideon: "If you have too many soldiers, when you win the battle, everyone will think you did it on your own. You may even be tempted to think so yourself."

The story doesn't tell us what Gideon thought about God's instructions. I can only imagine. And it probably can't be repeated in a G-rated book. Whatever it was, he kept it to himself, obeyed the Lord, and sent half his army packing.

Then God said, "Come to think of it, that's still too many. Take the soldiers you have left down to the river and tell them to take a drink of water. Send home anyone who uses his hands as a cup." In other words, God said, send home all the ones with half a brain. God let Gideon keep the guys who didn't have more sense than a carrot, the ones who knelt down and slurped the water up with their tongues. Gideon went to battle with three hundred men. Now, this isn't how anybody in his right mind would choose to do it. But Gideon and his band of dimwits won the day—God's upside-down way.

This battle, by the way, is the one the prophet Isaiah was remembering when he said, "The people who walked in darkness have seen a great light. . . . For the yoke of their burden, and the bar across their shoulders, the rod of their oppressor, you have broken as on the day of Midian" (Isa. 9:2, 4).

Sound familiar? It does if you have ever been to worship in a congregation that uses the lectionary (a common set of Scripture passages assigned for each Sunday and used by many mainline denominations) during the Advent and Christmas seasons. And the passage works during this upside-down season, because what could be more upside down than three hundred defeating one hundred thousand except this: God became a human being and chose to show up in the form of a tiny infant.

Could anything be more upside down than that?

Well, okay, I can think of one thing. It is the most upside-down thing of all: the cross on which the Son of the Most High, the Lord of lords, and the living word of God was killed.

And that, finally, is what a "theology of the cross" is all about. The cross is our constant reminder that we have been created, claimed, and called by a God who is, well, *weird*. God does the undoable. Thinks the unthinkable. Loves the unlovable. Forgives the unforgivable. Saves the unsavable. And God does it in the strangest way possible. God comes to us in the face of a stranger, a convicted criminal, a reject, a failure, an upside-down Messiah. This is how God works.

The cross is our reminder that, as soon as we start thinking we can figure it all out, anticipate God's next move, and capture God in our theological constructs, we are as far away from getting it right as we could be. As soon as we think we have all the answers, we certainly don't.

Case in Point

The Bible can be—and has been—a dangerous weapon when wielded by people and churches who think they have all the answers.

For example, in answer to the question, "What does God want?" some Christians today are absolutely certain the biblical answer is: "Get with the program. Shape up or ship out. Behave yourself or you're doomed to eternal damnation." No wonder the Good News so often sounds bad.

The street preacher in my neighborhood is a case in point. He has been working the same corner for more than three decades. Every day all summer long, he stands on that corner with a microphone and a little amplifier at his feet. He watches the people passing by, taking his cues from them and whatever "vices" he judges them to have. And he preaches right at them. The message is always the same: "You can't smoke cigarettes [or drink alcohol or have premarital sex or whatever else he sees or imagines he sees in front of him] and get into heaven! The devil wants you to smoke cigarettes [or fill in the blank]," he shouts at startled shoppers, people on their lunch break, and unsuspecting out-of-town visitors. "But, as it says in the Bible, you've got to stop smoking cigarettes [or fill in the blank] if you want to go to heaven!"

My son does a wickedly funny impersonation. And I laugh along with him. But it's not really an amusing situation.[1] A couple of years ago a story about this Chicago icon appeared in our local paper. The reporter wrote, "When asked to put his preachings in a nutshell, he said, 'People should obey God and stick with the Scriptures' (which according to [his] interpretation, imply that women were put in the world to bear children, obey men and keep their yaps shut)."[2] Never mind that he has no income of his own and his wife goes to work every day to support their eight children. The writer reported this little tidbit with glee, of course. I'm sure this street preacher has the best of intentions, but unfortunately for many people who live in my neighborhood, this is what they are being led to think is the "Good News" Christians have to share. And frankly, the fact that he doesn't know he looks like a chump makes him the biggest chump of all.

Thankfully, the damage this street preacher does is probably minimal. Put his message, however, into the hands of someone who runs a multimillion dollar media empire, polish it up a little, and put the weight of a couple academic degrees behind it and you have a whole different situation.

More Than an Answer Book

The Bible is not meant to be an answer book. It is especially not meant to be used that way when it comes to history or science questions. But it is not really even very good at answering moral or "religious" questions. Just for fun, try finding an answer to the question,

"According to the Bible, is worship more pleasing to God if people are singing to organ music or to a rock band?" That question alone could start a riot in a lot of congregations I know. But, in the end, you would have to agree that there is no ready, clear-cut biblical "answer" to it. In fact, that is true about most of the really tough questions people are asking today. That's why even the smartest, most faithful Christians can't agree about the death penalty, stem-cell research, homosexuality, immigration.

This is frustrating to a lot of people, and it would be kind of nice, in a way, if the Bible would give us clear-cut answers to the questions we face today. It would be nice if the Bible was perfectly clear. Some religions do claim to have holy books like that: a Qur'an transmitted literally from God by way of the angel Gabriel; the Book of Mormon, hidden on metal plates and magically translated by Joseph Smith. But, most Christian biblical scholars teach, "the Bible is no such book."[3] And what is even more frustrating is that the God who came to us in Jesus Christ intends for it to be this way.

The God we meet in the Old and New Testaments is madly in love with us and with our world (John 3:16). This love led God to risk coming to us in human form. God came to us in *Jesus* who, though without sin, was nevertheless really and truly human. Do you think that Jesus did not lose his temper? The Bible itself suggests that he did (Matt. 21:12-13). Do you think Jesus never had his heart broken, never felt his eyes fill up with tears that would not be stopped? The Bible actually describes it (John 11:35). Do you think that Jesus was never scared or anxious, never for a moment wished that God would do things differently and not ask so much of him? The Bible says otherwise (Luke 22:41-44). Do you think that Jesus did not experience thirst, did not feel alone, did not bleed? The Bible tells us he did (Matt. 27:45-50). In other words, the Bible tells us that although Jesus was fully God, he was also fully human.

In the same way, the Bible is a human book. It is not perfectly clear. And it was not handed down to us with a built-in search engine that would spit out simple answers seconds after we typed in our toughest questions. It is so much more than that. The Bible is the story of

God's loving mission throughout all of history to bless, save, set free, and reconcile the whole creation. It is a story. And within this story are eye-witness accounts of events that really happened. There are great, soaring myths that speak truths too great to tell any other way. There are parables, prophecies, and poems. There are sermons and there are songs.

What makes the Bible holy, what makes it *scripture* is that it points us to Jesus Christ. And so, at its core, the Bible is a love story. You might say that the heart of the biblical story beats with God's saving love, through Christ, for us and for our world. Martin Luther's much repeated phrase is much repeated because it is so helpful: "The Bible is the manger in which the word of God is laid."

As frustrating as this may sometimes be, the Bible does not tell us what we need to *know*. Rather, the Bible introduces us to the one who knows us. Neither is the Bible to be "obeyed." But we dare not ignore it, either, because as we read and wrestle with the Bible by the power of the Holy Spirit, it is Jesus Christ himself who meets us.

And Jesus has something to say.

The Bible on Center Stage

In fact, Jesus has something to say *to* us. And he has something to say *through* us to the world. To be "in" the scriptures is to be in conversation with the living word. And being in that conversation is an essential characteristic of the evangelical life.

It came as no surprise to me as we visited those growing congregations that people were enthusiastically committed to being in that conversation. We heard again and again in our interviews about the centrality of the Bible in their life together and in their individual lives.

In fact, one pastor at Blessed to Be a Blessing Lutheran Church was adamant on this point. Near the end of his interview, he said, "We're fanatical in some ways about the authority of scripture. Don't monkey with it. Don't tell me the gospel is something other, because it's not. It's the power of God to change lives. We will not budge on this."

People told us there is a high value on reading and studying scripture in their congregations. At Changed Lives Lutheran Church, for example, people are encouraged to read the Bible from start to finish. And, according to one lay leader, people have genuinely taken this to heart. They are looking for a connection with Jesus Christ, he believes, and for a connection with one another. Church members talk to one another about the process and share with one another about where they are in their discovery. Everyone is allowed to go at his or her own pace. There is no pressure, but, he added, "there was a big buzz in the church" because everyone is reading the Bible and has "these connection points" to talk about. Similarly, at Blessed to Be a Blessing, people are encouraged to engage in serious study. According to a young couple we spoke with who were new members of the congregation, more than five hundred people at a time are taking part in an adult educational program designed to introduce new believers and nonbelievers to Christianity. They said this program is a great way to see how the church operates and what the church believes in. They said specifically that this program dispels any myths that it is okay to "pick and choose from the Bible." People come to understand, they added, that the congregation has a "backbone" when it comes to the Bible, and this creates a real, emotional connection to the ministry there.

Also deeply significant to the people we talked with is that there is what they perceived as Bible-based preaching. One of the lay staff members at Changed Lives said that in his preaching, the senior pastor bases things on Scripture and makes it applicable to people's lives. The preaching at Changed Lives, he said, contextualizes the stories of the Bible into everyone's lives today, as well as offering a historical perspective so that people can understand biblical times.

But Scripture is not just preached, read, or even studied in these congregations. According to the people we met, it shapes their life together in profound ways. For, example, two lay leaders at Alleluia described the way people in the congregation deal with differences of opinion. One of them said, first, people are in constant communication with God. And in the midst of disagreement, leaders use a combination of prayer, silence, discussion, and Bible study. The other added, "It's amazing, and it works, and you can really see the hand of God at work." Similarly, at Changed Lives, one member told us "everything" is

Bible-based. The senior pastor particularly, she said, sets this tone in the way in which he can tell you where any issue the congregation faces is addressed in scripture.

Perhaps the most interesting thing I discovered as I listened to the people in these congregations describe the central role of the Bible in their life together is that their encounter with the word has led them to make *risky* moves, even when it has gotten them in trouble with denominational authorities. The senior pastor at Blessed to Be a Blessing described being told by judicatory leaders that a decision they made was "not Lutheran." He said what they had done had the potential of getting them "kicked out of the ELCA." They were worried about this, he said, but took the risk anyway because, at the end of the day, they believed Martin Luther himself "would smile on it theologically." Martin Luther, the pastor told me, was "radical." And by that he meant that Luther based his decisions "on the Bible" and what he heard the Lord saying to him.

People Shaped by the Word

Notice I haven't said anything about the *content* of the "biblical" teaching or preaching that was happening in any of these congregations. Truthfully, what I hear God saying through the scriptures is very different in many ways from what the pastors of these congregations are teaching and what most of the members are probably hearing. But I do believe the people in these congregations are being shaped by the word of God.

The truth is that when Christians read the written word of God, the living word of God always shows up. In other words, Jesus shows up. Jesus shows up when we read the Bible no matter what method of interpretation we are using, whether we take a literal, a historical-critical, or a narrative approach—or we are so new to the whole thing that we don't know what approach we should take and are busy just trying to figure out how to pronounce all the strange names. Jesus shows up in spite of all the prejudices and cultural biases we bring to our reading of the text. Jesus shows up regardless of whatever our political, moral, or theological agenda might be.

And he shapes us. Turning to the Scriptures and expecting to hear a word from Christ is risky business. We are met there by the one who knows everything there is to know about us. Our brokenness and our sin, our need and our failures cannot be hidden from him. There is no fooling him about anything, in fact. When Christ comes to meet us in the word, we are confronted by the depth of our unworthiness. But we are always loved. We are loved beyond imagination and beyond deserving, without limit, without condition. And we are always called, compelled even, to share this amazing love with everyone. I believe that one of the reasons the congregations we visited are characterized by such evangelical fervor is because people there are daring to risk this encounter with God through Scripture.

Likewise, I believe a lack of enthusiasm for the biblical story is one of the reasons so many mainline congregations today are floundering. It isn't just that so often Bible studies are poorly attended or that the "opening devotions" that begin our business meetings are so anemic. It's that too few people *think* in terms of the biblical stories. We haven't developed a habit of using the biblical stories as a lens for understanding our own lives and contexts. Most important, we haven't learned how to listen for the voice of a living God who has spoken—and who is still speaking—to us through these stories. In fact, many of us don't even realize that is what's happening.

Well, shame on us.

Martin Luther, who was himself born anew through an encounter with the living word, wrote:

> One thing, and only one thing, is necessary for Christian life, righteousness, and freedom. That one thing is the most holy word of God, the gospel of Christ, as Christ says, John 11 [25], "I am the resurrection and the life; he who believes in me, though he die, yet shall he live." . . . Let us then consider it certain and firmly established that the soul can do without anything except the word of God and that where the word of God is missing there is no help at all for the soul. If it has the word of God, it is rich and lacks nothing since it is the word of life, truth, light, peace, righteousness, salvation, joy, liberty, wisdom, power, grace, glory, and of every incalculable blessing.[4]

The people in the congregations we visited dare to expose themselves to God's living word. This has helped produce an evangelical explosion among them. They have been met by Jesus! And they do not doubt for a minute that their job is to share Jesus with their neighbors.

A Vital Word

I wonder what would happen if people in more of our congregations dared to take this risk. I'm not just talking about doing more "Bible study," although that would be a good start in many places. I'm talking about waking up to a vital word, one that shapes every aspect of our life together.

Is this possible? Well, frankly, I'm not sure. Too many of us in mainstream churches seem determined to fight with one another to the bitter end over what we think *the Bible* is saying instead of listening together for what we believe *God* is saying through the biblical story. On the other hand, I can't say enough about the power of these three simple questions for helping people learn to listen for God's voice through the Scriptures: (1) What do you see God doing in this story? (2) What do you hear God saying to you personally in this story? (3) What do you hear God saying to us as a congregation in this story?[5] I have seen people come alive because they have been courageous enough to dive into the Bible, asking questions like these. I have seen congregations resurrected because their leaders have dared to let questions like these—and the answers they have heard together—set the agenda and plot the course for them. I believe that a willingness to wrestle with questions like these, as we learn to listen for God's voice together, is one key to reclaiming the "E" word. After all, to be evangelical people is to have a good word to share with others. And how can that word come *through* us unless it has first come *to* us?

We will, of course, need to be careful as we listen together for God's voice through the biblical story. That means being honest as we dive in about the "agendas" we are bringing with us. We can never forget that, when it comes right down to it, we are all chumps trying to make sense of our upside-down God. But the promise is that Jesus even comes to chumps. He comes with love.

And he comes with a call.

Wrestling with the Word

1. The Gospel writer John tells us that Jesus the word of God "became flesh" (1:14). And in the last few chapters of John's Gospel, we are told that not even death can stop this word. Jesus is alive! Read John 20:1-28. What does this story tell us about the power of God's word? What does it say about who this word is "for"? What does it say about how this word gets spread? What do you hear God saying to you in this story?

2. There may be no more dramatic example of how the word of God comes to us and through us to others than in the story of the call of the prophet Ezekiel. We are told that Ezekiel actually eats the word and is then given the job of speaking that word to his fellow Israelites. Read Ezekiel 2:1—3:11. Have you ever experienced being "filled up" by God's word? When? Have you ever shared God's word with someone and been rejected for it? What happened? Why do you think God keeps speaking to us even though we sometimes refuse to hear?

Thinking Things Through

1. What role does the Bible play in your life? How about in the life of your congregation? Do people worship it? Argue about it? Ignore it? Manipulate it? Or do they really try to listen for what God is saying to them through it? What can you do to help people learn to expect God to speak to them through the Bible so that God can speak through them to others?

2. What do you think about this idea that, although God speaks to us through the Bible, it isn't "perfect"? Does this make you uncomfortable? Or does it set you free to engage the Bible in a whole new way?

3. When you are in a Bible study at your congregation, which of these things do people say more often: "I think this text is saying . . ." or "I think I hear God saying . . ."? What's the difference? Which of these are you more likely to say? Why? Which do you think is more likely to help us make decisions, take risks, and learn to confidently share our faith with others?

Talking It Over

Dear God, thank you for the way you keep speaking to us even when our hearts are hard and we close our ears to your good news. Help us to hear you! Teach us to listen. Give us courage to risk a life-changing encounter with your living word for the sake of all those who haven't heard the good news yet. In Jesus' name, amen.

4

Waking Up to Purposeful Life

Some people collect stamps. (No, scratch that. Nobody collects stamps anymore. I don't even think my kids know what stamps are. The only mail they know about has a different "E" in front of it.) Let's try this again. . . .

Some people collect shoes. Some people collect antique toys. Some people collect MySpace friends. Some people collect electronic gadgets.

I collect "aha!" moments.

In my travels, which often take me from one church conference to another, I get to hear a lot of stories. That's how people respond to things they hear me say or something I've written that they happened to read. They pull me to the side for a few minutes and tell me stories about things that have happened to them, ideas they have had, books they would like to write, dreams God has planted in them, prayers that have been answered, miracles they have seen. My favorites are the aha! moment stories. I write those down in a little journal I carry around. And if I don't have my notebook with me, I write it on whatever I can find. I have file folders at home full of scrap paper and old napkins, and I use these stories in articles, books, or sermons. They remind me that God teaches and transforms us in all kinds of ways, through all kinds of situations and people.

For example, on a sheet torn from someone's legal pad, I have a story about a pastor I met a few years ago. We were at a conference together, and I was teaching about what it means for people to stop *going* to church so that they can really *be* the church whenever we gather and wherever we go. During the break, I grabbed a cup of coffee—and he grabbed me.

"So," he said without a preface and without even introducing himself, "I've been leading this men's Bible study group for years. And for years, Clarence has been there every single week. Without fail. He's the most consistent member of the group. Then all of a sudden he doesn't show. It's Wednesday morning and Clarence is not there. I just thought, well, everybody needs a break once in a while. But the next week he didn't show either. I didn't want to make him feel guilty, so I didn't call him, but I was a little worried. Finally, when he didn't show up a third week in a row, I gave him a call.

"Clarence," I said, "what's going on? Is everything okay?"

"Sure," he said, "everything's okay with me. But about a month ago one of my buddies lost his wife. Nobody saw it coming. One day she was fine. The next day she was dead. Just like that. Boom. He is still reeling from it. Anyway, he and his wife had a tee time every Wednesday morning. And so now, on Wednesday mornings," Clarence explained, "I'm hanging out with him instead."

The storyteller paused at this point, looking at me as if that was all he was going to say. "Wait a minute," I said, "why are you telling me this story?"

He just laughed. "Don't you get it?" he said. "That was the first time in my whole ministry that I really understood something. The point of it all isn't getting guys to come to Bible study. The point of getting them to come to Bible study is what they're doing with the life they have out there."

Jesus Has Left the Building

This is a shockingly new and strange idea for too many of us who spend the majority of our time working within the institutional church. But it has to be one of the most bizarre twists in history that a religion founded by the followers of an itinerant preacher came to be so "walled in." The way Jesus' story is told in the Bible, this was the last thing he would have wanted.

Listen to how the Gospel writer Matthew tells how Jesus began his public ministry:

Now when Jesus heard that John had been arrested, he withdrew to Galilee. He left Nazareth and made his home in Capernaum by the sea, in the territory of Zebulun and Naphtali, so that what had been spoken through the prophet Isaiah might be fulfilled:

> "Land of Zebulun, land of Naphtali,
>   On the road by the sea, across the Jordan, Galilee of the Gentiles—
> the people who sat in darkness
>   have seen a great light,
> and for those who sat in the region and shadow of death
>   light has dawned."

From that time Jesus began to proclaim, "Repent, for the kingdom of heaven has come near." (4:12-17)

Right from the very beginning, it was clear that Jesus would not easily be institutionalized. Think about this: back in his day, religious people had all kinds of ideas about who the "Messiah" would be and what he would do when God finally sent him. They had a whole long list of things they wanted him to take care of: old scores they wanted him to settle, enemies they wanted him to destroy, blessings they wanted him to bestow. But Jesus—the Lord of lords and King of kings—would not be molded by human hands, limited by our imaginations, or walled in by our expectations. The town in which Jesus chose to kick off his ministry wasn't Jerusalem, the obvious choice, the religiously acceptable and expected choice. Instead, unexpectedly, Jesus started his ministry in Capernaum, a rough-and-tumble seaport town located right in the middle of "Galilee of the Gentiles." It was there, not in a temple or on a sacred mountain or in a holy city, but rather standing at the crossroads of the nations, that Jesus announced, "The kingdom of heaven has come near!" (Mark 1:14).[1]

According to Matthew, it was there in Capernaum and in the region called Galilee, in a sort of church with no walls, that Jesus did many of the miracles and preached many of the sermons he is most famous for. It was in Galilee that he called those first startled disciples (Matt. 4:18-22) and healed Peter's mother-in-law, thereby no doubt putting Peter in her good graces for the rest of his life and setting the bar impossibly high for every son-in-law to follow (8:14-15). It was there that Jesus taught the scribes a thing or two about the Sabbath (12:1-14), called the twelve apostles (10:1-4), and delivered the Sermon on the Mount to rapt crowds who may or may not have had any idea that they had ringside seats to the most earthshaking event in history (5–7). In other words, Jesus did most of the really important stuff "out there" where real people live, work, and hang out instead of "in here" where we religious people would expect him to be.

Those of us who spend our days eating, sleeping, and breathing institutional air are prone to forget that Jesus does not live inside these four church walls of ours. In fact, *Jesus has left the building.* That doesn't mean Jesus isn't "in here" when we gather to swap stories about how we have seen God at work "out there" and to share his Supper with each other and to encourage and equip each other for the evangelical mission to which God has called us. But when Jesus calls us to follow him, he is calling us to follow him to the crossroads—into the places where we work, go to school, and play; into our neighborhoods; and into our homes.

Nurturing a Priesthood of All Believers

I confess that when I was serving as a parish pastor, I really didn't get the concept of nurturing a priesthood of believers. Well, maybe I got it a little. But my main focus, for most of my congregational ministry, was on getting people into the church building. And I wasn't too bad at that. But, frankly, that wasn't really all that hard to do. The harder and infinitely more interesting challenge is this: how can we create a culture "in here" that makes what happens "out there" the most important thing? I believe one of the reasons the congregations we studied are growing so dramatically is that they are taking this question seriously.

To be sure, the people we talked to did describe all the ways in which ministry is shared by everyone *inside* their congregations. We asked one woman, "Why do you think this congregation is growing?"

And she said, "We really do believe it's a God thing." But, she added, "It's also about the type of leadership we have. [Our senior pastor] is willing to delegate and willing to say it's not about him. It's his responsibility to empower people to do ministry. It's not his responsibility to do all the ministry." Some people admitted that this is just about being practical. In such enormous congregations, everyone has to be involved in something, because there is so much work to be done, which implies, I think rightly, that in smaller congregations it is too easy to assume that the pastor will "do everything." But the emphasis, at least on the part of the leaders we spoke with, is not on getting people involved in ministry inside the congregation. What they seem to be most interested in is getting people to see the opportunities and the responsibility they have to be in ministry outside the congregation.

Alleluia, for example, was in the middle of a six-week sermon series while we were there, using the theme "Promise and Purpose." During his message the day we visited, the preacher asked the congregation, "But what do you *do* with the gift [God gives you]?" He said, "We don't want to pack away God's love gift. He wants to live in our lives everyday." We receive God's promises and God's gifts, but they are not just for our own lives. They are for others, he said, "even for our enemies."

This message is not just preached at these congregations, however. The pastoral leaders at Alleluia told us that helping people embrace their call to ministry in their daily lives means making sure they are treated as ministers within the congregation too. One leader talked passionately about the centrality of the "priesthood of all believers" and added, "People are everything." He said he believes in nurturing grassroots ministries within the congregation. In fact, if anyone makes a suggestion that is in alignment with the mission, vision, and values of the congregation, he or she gets an easy green light. The leaders, he said, "rarely squash anything that people bring in."

Similarly, the senior pastor at Blessed to Be a Blessing told me that he believes the priesthood of all believers is a "bedrock piece" of what their Lutheran congregation is all about. Ministry belongs to the people, he said, explaining that ministry is "not just churchly but *kingdomly*. We are here so we can go out and build God's kingdom." At Blessed to Be a Blessing, people are encouraged to participate in the "9 to 5 window" they have for workplace ministry. One thousand people at Blessed to Be a Blessing signed up to receive regular e-mail messages designed to be spread to their workmates. The pastor added emphatically, "We're not just doing church around here. We're putting legs on it."

One of the pastors at Changed Lives Lutheran Church explained that his purpose on the staff is primarily designed to help people in the congregation figure out how God wants them to affect the world beyond the church walls. God wants us to "scatter the church," he said, and his job is to strategically place people where they can do their best. He also said that God has a purpose for us in the world, which is to bless people and to bring the presence of God to them. He said his job is to "get these five thousand people engaged outside these walls." And he added, "Joy is great, but if you never do anything, so what?"

One of the most memorable conversations I had during these visits illustrates exactly what this pastor was saying—and it occurred after the tape recorder was turned off. At Disciple Making Lutheran Church, one woman told me that she loves her congregation because they teach that we are saved by grace and there is nothing we have to do to earn our salvation. She emphasized that they are taught not to think they have to "work" for God's love. But, she said, this just makes her want to work for God. She explained that she is a hospital nurse and, as such, is often present at the time of death. She described what it is like to close off the body behind a curtain to gently clean and carefully prepare it to be visited by family or even just taken away for processing. This is the time, she said with tears in her eyes, when she is most aware of being God's hands in the world. And she tries to remember that this is always the case, in everything she does.

With stories like these, the people I talked to made the link between what they do inside and how they live outside of the congregation. One member of Alleluia told us that his congregation is rooted in spreading God's word and bringing people closer to God. "We're not just here for the social activities," he said. "What matters here is helping people feel a personal relationship with Jesus Christ. Once you get someone in that mode," he explained, "God's going to be talking through them.

And then it's a snowball effect. 'I want to go to Guatemala.' 'I want to do an inner-city ministry.' 'I want to do a construction ministry.'" He says he hears things like this on a weekly basis from people in his congregation and that it comes from their hearts, from their relationship with Christ.

One of the newest staff members at Changed Lives said she knows people from other congregations often criticize hers. One of the most hurtful and unfair criticisms, she said, is that they are preaching a "theology of glory" at Changed Lives. In other words, they are accused of teaching that if you know Jesus, you will be rich and famous. But she said that's just not true. The message at Changed Lives is this, she said: if you know Jesus, "you will want to tell your neighbor about it."

What Really Matters to God

The congregations we visited are very good at bringing people *in*. I believe that is, at least in part, because they are so very committed to encouraging and equipping people to be sent *out* for ministry. In other words, they understand the inviolable connection between the gift of our salvation and the call to follow Jesus into the crossroads of our daily lives. They understand that is the central purpose of the Christian life.[2]

That is how the apostle Paul puts it, anyway. He is the author of the words that sparked the Reformation five hundred plus years ago: "There is no distinction, since all have sinned and fall short of the glory of God; they are now justified by his grace as a gift through the redemption that is in Christ Jesus" (Rom. 3:22-24). We are saved, Paul says, by grace alone through faith in Christ! There is nothing we have to do to earn this. We have been "set free" (6:18). In chapter after chapter, Paul's letters ring out the freedom that is ours through Christ. But somewhere along the line in every letter there is a "so that."

Check it out: "Blessed be the God and Father of our Lord Jesus Christ," Paul writes to his friends in Corinth, "the Father of mercies and the God of all consolation, who consoles us in all our affliction, *so that* we may be able to console those who are in any affliction with the consolation with which we ourselves are consoled by God" (2 Cor. 1:3-4, emphasis added). "God is able to provide you with every blessing in abundance, *so that* by always having enough of everything, you may share abundantly in every good work" (2 Cor. 9:8, emphasis added).

Paul makes it clear that everything God does for us, God does *so that* we can be in service to others. "For you were called to freedom brothers and sisters," he teaches, "only do not use your freedom as an opportunity for self-indulgence, but through love become slaves to one another. For the whole law is summed up in a single commandment, 'You shall love your neighbor as yourself'" (Gal. 5:13).

When Martin Luther picked up Paul's call to freedom by grace through faith in Christ, he helped create a movement that shook the world. He also picked up on the "so that": "Although the Christian is thus free from all works," he said, "he ought in this liberty to empty himself, take upon himself the form of a servant, be made in the likeness of men, be found in human form, and to serve, help, and in every way deal with his neighbor as he sees that God through Christ has dealt and still deals with him."[3] In other words, through Christ, God sets us free

There is nothing we could ever do to earn or work our way "up" to God. God always "comes down" to save us and to set us free *so that* we can love and serve our neighbor![4]

from having to worry about "getting saved" by being good enough or by doing enough or by having the right kind of spiritual experience *so that* in freedom we can love and serve our neighbors. Simply put, Luther said we are set free *so that* we can serve.

And for God that is the bottom line. God is more interested in how we are serving our neighbor than in any other single thing. More than our prayer life. Certainly more than our sex lives. Even more than our worship life. And this, particularly, is worth thinking about, because my guess is that if you asked people, "What is the purpose of the Christian life?" a lot of them would answer, "To worship God." But that is not what God teaches us through the biblical story. As a matter of fact, our worship life has the capacity to really tick God off if we think that's what being a

Christian is all about. Read the Old Testament prophet Amos if you want the ugly details, especially Amos 5:21-24. Or check out what Jesus has to say about the scribes and Pharisees in Matthew 23. The bottom line for God is definitely not about how often or how beautifully we worship.

The point of the Christian life is what we do when we are "out there," as we follow Jesus to the crossroads, into our neighborhoods and into the world.

Following Jesus to the Crossroads

After all, the very first thing Jesus did after his big announcement that a new kingdom was at hand (translation: "*Everything* is about to change!") was to grab the first couple of guys he saw and say, "Hey, I want you to give me a hand." Notice what Jesus didn't say to those fishermen. He didn't say, "My children, come follow me to church" or "Men of Galilee, come follow me to a prayer meeting" or even " 'Sup dudes? Wanna do some Bible study?" Instead, Jesus called his disciples to follow him into a crazy, busy life of healing and teaching and proclaiming the good news of the kingdom everywhere they went and to anyone who would listen. When Jesus says, "Follow me," he is calling us to action. Jesus calls us to follow him into the crossroads, right into the middle of everyday life.

Disciples do get together for worship, of course, and for prayer and Bible study. But that's not the point. Disciples do those things because it equips and energizes them for the real work Jesus calls them to do in the real world—such as tearing down the walls that separate people from one another and from God; making peace, feeding the hungry and standing up for the powerless; and telling everyone we meet about Jesus. That is the purpose of the Christian life. And the purpose of the institutional church at every level, including the congregation, is equipping us to do it.

We often get this mixed up. At least one prophetic voice from the middle of the last century, however, boldly reminds us that Christ's call to follow him into an evangelical life, sharing the Good News with others in everything we say and do, comes first, and what we think of as "church" comes second. J. C. Hoekendijk, a twentieth-century evangelist, argued that as Jesus' followers did what they had been sent to do, church happened. The "church" didn't send people out to do justice and tell the story of Jesus. Jesus sent people. And the institution emerged as a gift from the Holy Spirit to support us in our calling.[5] The institutional church matters, but it is not the point. The institution is only important because it supports, challenges, equips, and encourages us as we answer the call to evangelical ministry in our daily lives.

Hoekendijk was a Dutch Reformed church historian and theologian who was the son of missionary parents. Although he served during the formative years of the World Council of Churches as the secretary of the Department of Evangelism, he was frustrated by what he said appeared to be one self-serving "evangelism" program after another. "To put it bluntly," he said, "the call to evangelism is often little else than a call to restore 'Christendom. . . .' And the sense of urgency [to do evangelism] is often nothing but a nervous feeling of insecurity, with the established church endangered; a flurried activity to save the remnants of a time now irrevocably past."[6] Hoekendijk, as you can imagine, didn't make many friends saying things like that. In fact, unlike the names of other "big" church leaders from that era, his has largely been forgotten.[7] But his critique of our all-too-often transparent attempts to prop up the institution by getting more people in the seats and more dollars in the plate is still painfully valid.

"Our God is not a temple dweller," Hoekendijk scolded. "In the strict sense of the word, he is not even a church god. He advances through time; ever again he lets the new conquer the old. He is not a God of the 'status quo,' but rather the Lord of the future, King of the history of the world."[8] In other words, the God who comes to meet us in Jesus Christ will not be walled in. God is on the loose in the world! Jesus is at the crossroads. And it is to the crossroads that we are called to follow.

A Purposeful Life

One of my hunches about troubled mainline denominations and mainstream congregations is that we have allowed ourselves to become so preoccupied by the imagined threat of our imminent demise, so unbalanced by the changing culture around us, and so intimidated by the seemingly omnipotent Religious Right, that we have become increasingly inwardly focused. We jealously guard our members' time, talent, and money. We discourage people, in subtle and not-so-subtle ways, from getting involved in their communities or giving "at the office." We almost obsessively insist that a "good" member is somebody who puts in a lot of seat time "at church," and we ignore the fact that most of the good works our folks do happen on their own—not on our—time. We forget that "the church" is not the point.

God is on a loving mission to bless, save, reconcile, heal, and set free the whole world. We are called to participate in that mission everywhere we go, in everything we do. This is the evangelical purpose of the Christian life. We are saved and set free from every single thing that would kill us if it could *so that* we can follow Jesus to the crossroads of our daily lives. At the crossroads, we are called to heal the sick, feed the hungry, stand with the marginalized, raise the dead, speak truth to power, break down the barriers that divide us from each other and from God, welcome the stranger, and tell everyone we meet about what God is up to in Jesus. Jesus is calling us to be his witnesses, in word and in deed—in the places where we live and work, in our neighborhoods and in our classrooms, in the voting booth, in the blogosphere, and in the way we use our bank accounts.

Jesus is calling us, when necessary, to spend a quiet Wednesday morning comforting a grieving friend.

And now, let the people say, "Aha!"

Wrestling with the Word

1. Is the "so that" a new idea for you? It is for a lot of Christians who are used to thinking about their faith as all gift. But the gift of salvation and freedom is also a call to service. Read Galatians 5:1-14. Why do you think Paul uses such strong, graphic language here? What do you hear God saying to you through these words? What are you hearing God call you to do?

2. Go back and read Matthew 4:12-22. These are two "stories" that aren't usually read together. What happens when you read this

passage as a single story? How is your life as a follower of Jesus like those of the first disciples? How is it different?

Thinking Things Through

1. What is "the point" of your congregation? Getting people in the doors? Or sending them out? How can you tell? Get specific. Give examples that support your answers.

2. What do "the crossroads" look like for you? In other words, where are you being called to follow Jesus every day? Where do you spend your time? How do you share the Good News in those places?

3. What have you been hearing God call you to do—or to say—out there? What would God be doing through you right now if you dared to answer that call? You have been set free to do it! What is getting in your way? Why are you letting it?

Talking It Over

Dear God, it is so easy for us to get mixed up! Forgive us when we forget that a call to serve our neighbor comes hand in hand with your gift of salvation, forgiveness, and freedom. Help us to answer that call. Plant that single purpose in our hearts and minds. Give us courage to follow Jesus to the crossroads. Amen.

5

Waking Up
to Our Common Call

During the Q & A time after a presentation I recently made, one man in the audience challenged me on something he thought he had heard me say.

"But what's wrong with tradition?" he asked defiantly. A murmur rumbled across the room, signaling support for the question.

"Absolutely nothing," I replied.

The murmuring stopped suddenly, my listeners startled by what sounded like an abrupt about-face, because I had spent the preceding hour calling into question almost every one of our hallowed customs and sacrosanct rules.

"There is nothing wrong with tradition," I continued, "unless we have made it our god."

This answer seemed to satisfy the brave soul who asked the question and quiet down the crowd. But later I thought of an even better response. I wish that, instead, I had said, "Well, it depends on which tradition we're talking about."

We can all think of really terrible things the church has done and/ or endorsed over the centuries, because "that's the way we've always done it," and even found theological and biblical justification for it. Go ahead. Make a list right now. But not all traditions are bad. In fact, there is growing evidence that many people in this high-tech culture are longing for the high touch of ancient rituals. Some "emerging" church planters and ministry leaders are responding to this need by dusting off the religious icons, incense burners, and prayer litanies that "contemporary" worship leaders long ago discarded. The common denominator these two distinct groups share, however, is a commitment to reaching new generations with the good news about God's love. In other words, they both put God's mission ahead of church tradition. And in some ways, that is our most important tradition.

Martin Luther and company illustrated that fact in a big way—they didn't call it "the Reformation" for nothing. But the tradition of upending tradition for the sake of God's loving mission to save, reconcile, and set free the whole creation can be traced all the way back at least as far as Jesus.

Troublemaking as Spiritual Discipline

The Gospel writer Mark isn't even through two chapters in his story before we see Jesus in a big showdown with the keepers of religious tradition. He and his disciples are discovered picking food on the Sabbath, a definite no-no according to their tradition. "What?" Jesus responds. "Am I supposed to let them go hungry?" The religious leaders are indignant and vow to keep their eye on this rule-breaking troublemaker.

The next time Jesus goes into the synagogue, he walks into a trap. A man there has a withered hand. Jesus knows the religious leaders are watching, waiting to catch him in the act of breaking their rules. "So," he says to them, "which is worse? Breaking the law because you're helping someone or breaking the law by letting him die?"

They don't respond. They don't dare. All they care about is piling up enough evidence to condemn him. Both saddened and angry at their hard hearts, Jesus turns away from them and toward the man who has been sitting there patiently listening to his future being debated.

"Give me your hand," Jesus commands.

In a blink the man is healed, about as long as it takes for the Pharisees and the Herodians to decide that this Jesus has to go. (The whole story is told in Mark 2:23—3:5.)

We have all been where the Pharisees were that day, right? *None* of us likes having our traditions messed with. But there is no tradition, no custom, no religious rule, no order, and no law—not even one such as the Sabbath, one instituted by God on high—that can take precedence over God's loving mission to bless, save, heal, reconcile, and set people free (Mark 2:27-28).

For those of us who follow Jesus, the only standard by which to measure the things we do is this: Does it serve our neighbor? Does it heal? Does it bless? Does it communicate the good news of God's limitless and unconditional love? Does it set people free? This is the standard Jesus himself used in his ministry. And it is the standard that guided those earliest Christians as they carried out Jesus' commandment to be his witnesses unto the ends of the earth.

No wonder even the most mild-mannered Christians are often so good at making trouble. In some ways, it is an ancient and honored spiritual discipline. Take, Philip, for example (Acts 8). He was in over his head, stuck out on a wilderness road, led there unexpectedly and inexplicably by the Spirit. All he had done was sign up to serve on a committee, the early church's first. He thought his job was simple: run the food pantry. But he and the rest of the Christians in Jerusalem had been run out of town after Stephen, a fellow committee member, had been outspoken enough about Jesus to get himself killed. Philip was, without a doubt, wondering what in the world he had gotten himself into, when suddenly a chariot appeared in the distance, kicking up dust, obviously in a hurry to get somewhere. What Philip didn't know is that inside the chariot sat a very important—and very unusual—man, in the service of the Ethiopian queen and her fortune. The chariot slowed when it got near Philip. Curious, Philip drew near enough to hear the man reading aloud from, of all things, the Jewish scriptures—we call them the Old Testament now, the Bible.

"Do you have any idea what this means?" the man asked when he saw Philip listening.

"Well, actually, yes I do," Philip said.

He climbed inside the chariot and explained everything he knew about Jesus, how God was pointing to Jesus all throughout those old stories, and how God's dream is for everyone in the world to be reconciled to one another and to God. The Ethiopian had never heard anything like this before. He wanted it—more than anything.

"Look!" he said, "there is some water. Baptize me!"

Now, at this point, all the color probably drained away from Philip's face. There were a half dozen really good reasons why this strange man could not and should not be baptized. But the biggest reason—and the thing the Jerusalem church leaders would be most upset about—was that the man wasn't circumcised. In fact, given that he was a eunuch—neutered, you might say, so that he wouldn't be tempted to "service" more than the queen's treasury—Philip wasn't sure he was even a "he." But he was quite sure the man wasn't Jewish. And up until that day, every Christian that Philip knew about had been a Jew first. That's how it had *always* been.

"What is to stop me from being baptized?" the man asked again.

And Philip, knowing he'd have some explaining to do when he got back home, apparently thought, *Well, nothing important enough to trump God's mission. Nothing bigger than the blessing God has planned for the whole world. Nothing greater than the freedom we have both been given through Christ.*

"Nothing I can think of," Philip said. "Let's do it."

Whatever It Takes

"Let's do it. Let's try it. Let's risk it."

Our common call as the church is to participate in God's loving mission to save the whole world—whatever it takes. Even if "whatever it takes" gets us into trouble.

For Jesus, "whatever it takes" meant doing a good deed for someone even though it was the Sabbath day. For Philip, "whatever it takes" meant accepting someone who wasn't Jewish into the Christian community. But it's hard to fully appreciate just how radical these decisions were from our twenty-first-century perspective. Think about it: Are either of these big issues for you and your friends today? Is anybody you know arguing that *only* Jewish people can become members of your congregation? I doubt it. And for most of us, even the idea of keeping the Sabbath seems old fashioned. Let's be honest. Even if we do participate in a worship service on the Sabbath (and, on average each week, only about 30 percent of all Christians do), most of us spend the rest of the day shopping or catching up on paperwork or taking in a movie—activities that would have been strictly outlawed within the religion of Jesus' day. Does anybody you know think pulling weeds after worship is sinful? I doubt that too. From our perspective, it's hard to understand why Philip or Jesus would have been in so much trouble. The things they were advocating seem like no big deal to us today. But don't forget: Jesus got killed for the trouble he caused. And his followers often didn't fare much better. The fact is, even when their actions endangered them, Jesus and his followers were willing to do whatever it took to get the good news out to people in their day.

What does "whatever it takes" look like today? What does it look like for you and your congregation? I know one tattooed pastor who puts on a T-shirt and blue jeans and hangs out at the local pool hall every weekend. He says he meets people there who would never show up for worship at his congregation on a Sunday morning. He says he has had some of his most meaningful conversations about Jesus happen over a beer on Saturday night. He knows he will never get elected bishop anywhere, and his congregational leaders aren't too sure how they feel about his methods, but he believes he is doing "whatever it takes."

Some congregational leaders I know discovered that the best way to share the good news with the people in their community, many of whom had been burned by "church" before and had become deeply suspicious of "the institution," was to have laypeople lead worship services, preach, and even preside at the Lord's Supper. It was the most powerful way they could think of to communicate that "church" is not a pastor or a building or a budget or a bunch of rules. The "church" is people—*real* people—all of whom have been called to share the good news about Jesus whenever they gather and wherever they go. They got into serious hot water with the judicatory leaders in their area (i.e., the bishop and his staff) in spite of the fact that their faith community was growing faster than just about any other congregation around. They believed they were doing "whatever it takes."

"We'll do whatever it takes to connect with people who may not be connected to God yet" is the refrain of a faith community that remembers it has been set free to serve and that puts neighbor first. This is what we sound like when God's dream of a world that has been healed, redeemed, and reconciled has set us loose to dream too. That is what it is like when the only standards we use in our life together are: Does it bless? Does it communicate God's unconditional love? Does it set people free?

Jesus' call to an evangelical life does not come just to each one of us. This is a call we share. God is on a loving mission to bless, save, reconcile, heal, and set free the whole world. And we have a call to participate in that mission everywhere we go, in everything we do. But a common call to be evangelical people does not have to mean conformity. In fact, what we need more than ever in mainstream congregations and across mainline denominations is the freedom to experiment, the permission to make gigantic messes trying new things, and the encouragement to respond to each new context with open minds and creative spirits. We need flexibility, not lock-step uniformity. We need innovation, not institutionalized sameness. We need faith enough to risk going in directions we have never gone before—even multiple directions at the same time!—not a fear-based clampdown on anything and everyone new. We need a willingness to do *whatever it takes*, change whatever needs changing, and fix whatever isn't working to answer Christ's call to share the Good News with everyone. We need to celebrate the role that faithful troublemakers play in our midst—both in our congregations and throughout the churchwide structures. I believe those sixteenth-century Protestant reformers, in whose shadow we stand, would wholeheartedly agree.

We Have Been Set Free

In January of 1526, as the Protestant Reformation was sweeping across Germany, evangelical (remember, that's what Lutherans were called) church leaders needed new tools and resources to help put their radical new Reformation ideas into action. That's why Martin Luther, busy trying not to get killed by an angry and outraged papacy, translated the Bible into German—the first time in history the Bible appeared in something other than Latin (which nobody knew how to read anymore) or Greek and Hebrew (the original biblical languages, also not widely understood in sixteenth-century Europe!). He also produced educational materials, including the Large and Small Catechisms, to help children and adults learn the basics of their faith from this new evangelical perspective. And he was prevailed upon to write a new "mass," a worship service that would reflect the theological concepts and biblical insights that sparked the Reformation in the first place.

That's when Dr. Luther started getting nervous. He fretted that if he wrote a new mass and everyone started using it, people might get the idea they were supposed to use this mass forever. He agreed to do it anyway, recognizing that pastors needed help moving their congregations into a new day. But in the "Preface to the German Mass and Order of Divine Service," he said as clearly as he was able, "No order [of worship] has any intrinsic worth of its own." He introduced the new mass by saying, "Above all things, I most affectionately and for God's sake beseech all, who see or desire to observe this our Order of Divine Service, on no account to make of it a compulsory law, or to ensnare or make captive thereby anyone's conscience; but to use it agreeably to Christian liberty at their good pleasure as, where, when and so long as circumstances favour and demand it."[1] In other words, Luther said, when it's not working anymore, change it! If you have something better, use it! If, in your context, you think you can design something that will be more appropriate, do it!

Our worship services—and anything else we do, for that matter—should always and everywhere be conducted within the context of Christian freedom. We are, Luther argued, absolutely and completely free from all legalistic orders and traditions in every part of our life together. We are bound, Luther said, by one thing and one thing only: service to our neighbor. This is the only standard we should use to measure everything we do. It is not just the "gold" standard; it is the only standard. And what our neighbors need above all else, Luther explained, is the good news that Jesus came to bring.

So, in the case of our worship forms and orders, Luther explained that the purpose is "the promotion of faith and the service of love."[2] In other words, the point of our worship services is not to satisfy our aesthetic tastes, to fulfill some holy requirement, or even (and here's where Luther gets really radical) to "worship God." The whole point of "the service" is to teach and equip us—sinners all, and especially "the simple, unbelievers, and the young"—to be a part of God's mission in the world. Luther makes this point forcefully: the "object" of our worship service is not God. God is the subject of the service. And we, the people who are participating in the service, are the objects. The message, the singing, the readings—everything is done with *us* in mind—to teach us and equip us so that, as he put it, we "may become conversant with Scripture and expert in its use, ready and skillful in giving an answer for [our] faith, and able in time to teach others and aid in the advancement of the kingdom of Christ."[3]

Ideally, Luther said, we would have a whole variety of worship services. He suggested three. First, he said, perhaps surprisingly, keep the Latin mass. Why? Because it would teach us a foreign language! And this, he said, would be helpful when we are sharing the Good News with those who don't speak our language. "I would gladly," he wrote, "raise up a generation able to be of use to Christ in foreign lands and to talk to their people."[4] Second, he said, offer a service in the native language of the people, especially for the sake of those who are "not yet believers or Christians" as a "public allurement to faith and Christianity."[5] In other words, he encouraged, don't make them learn your language or customs. Use their language, customs, and means of communication so that they can understand what you are saying. Third, and most dramatically, Luther says the "true type of Evangelical Order," the ideal service, would be a house church. Here's how he describes it:

> Those . . . who are desirous of being Christians in earnest, and are ready to profess the Gospel with hand and mouth, should register their names and assemble by themselves in some house to pray, to read, to baptize and to receive the sacrament and practice other Christian works. . . . Here there would not be need of much fine singing. Here we could have baptism and the sacrament in short and simple fashion: and direct everything towards the word and prayer and love.[6]

Even as Luther was writing a new worship service that he knew would be used by congregations across Germany, he was teaching that there is not one right way to do things in the church . . . not even something as central as the worship service. We are completely free from all traditions and legalistic orders. The only measure in everything we do is this: Are we serving our neighbor? Are we teaching and showing them how to be Christians and how to live the Christian life? Are we inviting them to participate in God's mission to love, bless, reconcile, set free, and save the world? Are we being Christ to them?

Passion Inspires Risk-taking

Perhaps nothing was more readily apparent to me as I studied those sample congregations than their absolute dedication to reaching their neighbors for the sake of teaching and showing them how to be Christians and how to live the Christian life. In fact, the desire to connect with people who do not know Jesus and are not yet a part of any faith community appears to drive everything that happens in these congregations. For the sake of reaching new people, these congregations seem ready to try anything.

One lay member of the leadership team at Blessed to Be a Blessing characterized his congregation as an outward moving church. The members themselves, he said, draw people in. "They've caught the vision of Blessed to Be a Blessing," he said. "They really believe what we're doing here is of value and really helps the kingdom of God." He says they "own the vision [of the congregation] and run with it." He added, "This church doesn't sit." Their senior pastor tells them he "doesn't want to seek ten thousand. He wants to send ten thousand." The people at Blessed to Be a Blessing believe there are people who need what they have to offer, and they want to reach out to them.

We heard a very similar story from people across the board, both clergy and lay, at each congregation we visited. Blessed to Be a Blessing has a pastor on its staff whose full-time job is "invitation." He explains that his starting point in ministry is Luke 15. This is where Jesus tells three stories about people losing things: the sheep, the silver coin, and the son. These stories, he said, exemplify Christ's heart to reach out to people. It is the "ticking heart of God." Repeating an oft-used quote, he said, "The Church is the only institution in the world that exists for its nonmembers." And he added, "We need to be fully outwardly focused in order to engage in the mandate of the Great Commission."

At Changed Lives, the youth director talked throughout his entire interview about getting kids to invite their friends to church. He described a growing confirmation and preconfirmation children's program. The kids and youth, he said, want to be a part of spreading the good news. Similarly, the lay president of the congregation described their dream for doing "church plantings" to the west of the congregation and in the north suburbs of their town. He told us that 65 percent of their neighbors are not connected to a faith community yet and that Changed Lives wants to reach these people. He knows that some of their members believe the congregation is already too big, but he responds to this concern by saying, "Is everyone in [this community] part of a church now? If not, then we're not too big." Most people, though, are excited about the plan to spawn new congregations. In fact, he told us there are hundreds of Changed Lives members who are ready and willing to move out and start new churches.

Reflecting on the enthusiasm for reaching new people that permeates Changed Lives, one staff member told us, "I personally feel there are congregations . . . that don't have a clear vision of what God would want for them, that don't know God has so much more passion for them than they understand." She explained, it's not that God wants every congregation to be "snazzier and bigger," but that Christ "weeps for these people who have so much more life to live . . . and so much more of an opportunity to give that witness to other people." God is pleased whenever people come together for worship, she acknowledged. But God "is so much bigger than that. His purpose is to redeem the world, and so when we're not about that, what are we doing?"

Each congregation regularly offers a variety of educational, service, and social programs designed specifically to attract newcomers. At Blessed to Be a Blessing, one night a week is dedicated to "kindness ministry." People in need from the community are invited in for a meal.

Counseling is available to them at no charge. Free haircuts are given. And more. "[When you] consider kindness ministry for those who are far away [from God, it's about] being the good news rather than speaking the good news." Eventually, he said, people want to know, "What does the gospel say? What does it mean for us?"

We were actually able to attend what is called a "garage door" event at Changed Lives Lutheran Church. Over six thousand people attended outdoor worship services, ate served free hot dogs and hamburgers, and enjoyed fun and games. Members of the congregation had been encouraged to bring friends and neighbors who didn't have a church home. "If it was two people, I'd think it was successful," one staff member said. "If it's ten people, great. Then, for those ten people, we're delivering God's message of grace and hope. It just happens to be six thousand here." She believes that the members at Changed Lives are meeting a God who wants to transform them. And once they know that, they go and tell other people. "We couldn't possibly conceive of a marketing campaign to bring in what you saw out there tonight," she said. "All we did was put a postcard in their bulletins [that] said, 'Invite a coworker, invite a friend, invite your neighbors.'"

One of the most obvious ways that we saw this desire to reach new people expressed was in the various styles of worship offered in each congregation. One of the pastors at Blessed to Be a Blessing was adamant that anything that prevents people from feeling welcomed into the presence of God is wrong. "If we make the mistake that [the formalities of traditional worship] are irrevocably tied to truth in this form, then we cut ourselves off from reaching people."

Although each of these congregations offered a variety of what would be called "contemporary" or "emerging" styles of worship, none of them seemed tied to any particular form. At Changed Lives, one member explained they have the traditional "LBW" (*Lutheran Book of Worship*) service at which "[the senior pastor] gets dolled up in the stole." They also have "Sunday morning praise worship, come-as-you-are Saturdays, and an emerging service on Thursday," which she described as a "headbanger service that serves the younger crowd" but which, in spite of the volume, is actually rooted in ancient rituals being resurrected for use in a new day. Another member of Changed Lives described the standard they use for the worship services they offer. He said, "If people's lives change, that's cool. That's what we're here for."

In their willingness to try anything for the sake of reaching new people, the leaders of these congregations believe they are living out the ideas preached by those sixteenth-century Reformers. One leader commented that, although many Lutherans want the worship service to be identical anywhere in the country, that's "silly." Martin Luther, she said, "was the ultracontextual guy, and we've made his church [in too many other places] into a noncontextual church." She believes Luther would be very happy at her congregation. "He'd probably be playing electric guitar in the band."

Our Common Call

As heirs of the Reformation, we do, in fact, have a tradition of upending tradition for the sake of our call to participate in God's loving mission to save and set free the world. But it is natural, when threatened, to start making rules and calling for everyone to get on the same page.

That's why, for example, the management program called Six Sigma is so popular in the business world these days. In fact, it has been implemented in eighty-five of the top one hundred U.S. corporations over the past decade or so, and it continues to infatuate business leaders across the nation who are desperate, in the face of a changing and uncertain economy, to decrease production defects and increase efficiency.

But recently there have been some pretty brutal critiques of the Six Sigma program. One writer, in particular, has zeroed in on the impact this approach to management has had on the famously creative culture at 3M, where Post-it™ notes and other marvels of modern life were hatched. The bottom line: Six Sigma, with its lock-step DMAIC (define, measure, analyze, improve, control) approach to eliminating unpredictability and demanding immediate and measurable results, sucks the life out of people and crushes creativity.

Six Sigma was brought to 3M in 2000 by a new CEO. The first thing he did was layoff eight thousand workers—about 11 percent of 3M's workforce. Then he intensified the performance review process and tightened the purse strings. Among other things, this meant ending 3M's longtime practice of encouraging its employees to use 15 percent of their time doing their own thing and pursuing independent projects. Wall Street loved it. The company's stock jumped 20 percent. And within four years the new CEO, now famous for bringing "discipline" to a company that observers said had become erratic and unwieldy, was offered an even bigger job as CEO of Boeing.

Well, he's gone, and, although he may be winning accolades again in his new position, his successor is cleaning up the mess at 3M. The once innovative company hasn't had a fresh idea in years. In the good old days, at least one-third of their sales were from products that had been invented in the past five years. Today that fraction is one quarter and slipping.

Art Fry is the 3M scientist who invented Post-it™ notes. He says, "Innovation is a numbers game. You have to go through 5000 to 6000 raw ideas to find one successful business." But that is exactly the kind of chaotic process Six Sigma is designed to "fix." The new CEO at 3M, George Buckley, says that invention cannot happen "in that atmosphere of confinement or sameness. Perhaps one of the mistakes that we made as a company—it's one of the dangers of Six Sigma—is that when you value sameness more than you value creativity, I think you potentially undermine the heart and soul of a company."

Quietly, the Six Sigma legacy is being transformed at 3M. One member of the 3M team says, "I feel like we can dream again."

I wonder what we in mainstream Christianity need to do—or stop doing—in order for us to start dreaming again. I don't know about you, but I am ready for it.

We have a call to answer.

Wrestling with the Word

1. Read the Great Commandment (Matt. 22:34-40) and the Great Commission (Matt. 28:16-20) together. What do you hear God saying to you through these words? What do you hear God saying to your faith community? What are you going to do about that?

2. In the story of Peter and Cornelius, God breaks God's own laws! Read that story in Acts 10–11. What laws does God tell Peter to break? What is Peter's reaction? What is God trying to tell Peter? What happens? What can we learn from this?

Thinking Things Through

1. This chapter argues that "our common call as the church is to participate in God's loving mission to save the whole world—whatever it takes." What do you think about that? Is this how most people in your faith community would describe their "purpose" as the church? Can you think of a recent decision or action by your faith community that reflected God's purpose? Can you think of one that didn't?

2. What would be different in your faith community if the only standard you used to make decisions, create programs, offer services, plan worship, build buildings, choose staff, and do every other thing you do was "Does it serve our neighbor?" What would you do that you are not doing now? What would you stop doing?

3. How much do you dislike taking risks, trying new things, and generally upending tradition? How much less would you dislike it if you really believed that God has set us free from bondage to rules *so that* we can love and serve our neighbor? How can you give people in your faith community permission to embrace that freedom and act as if they are really free? What would you do if you really believed you are free?

Talking It Over

Dear God, we are sinful people and we belong to broken communities. Nevertheless, you choose to work through us and call us to be a part of your mission in this world. What a great gift that is! Thank you for this call. It has changed our lives! Help us to embrace it. Give us courage to live in the freedom that is ours as we answer it. Make us willing to go anywhere, do anything, and risk everything for the sake of sharing your Good News with our neighbors. Amen.

6

Waking Up
to Transformational Power

"Have you ever worked with towns that are in a state of upheaval, stress, and divisiveness?"

That's how the frantic e-mail message I received a few months ago began. The writer, a Sunday school teacher in her congregation and a mother of two, was desperate. She and her husband had attended a town council meeting the night before where fistfights had been broken up by local police and arrests had been made.

"Basically," she wrote, "this is a small town near a popular vacation spot. It has experienced major growing pains in the past several years, more than doubling its population."

Hers was a familiar story in many ways. Some of the old-timers in town don't like the growth and are doing what they can to stop it. But for some people in this town it has become personal. A few have developed a sort of school-yard bully mentality. People think nothing of making personal attacks on one another. And the community is coming apart at the seams.

"I love this town," she said, "and the people in it, and I can't stand to see this happening. I want us all to get past this, and I want this town to be able to heal. Can you help?"

I wrote back right away to encourage her and also to say that I could only be helpful if the town leaders invited me to be. But by the time she received my response, she had already pulled herself together.

"I feel," she wrote back, "like maybe this is why I was put in this position, and maybe I can be a catalyst for positive change in this town. I may seek help in this from others in my church—I think it would be a really groundbreaking project for us." Her congregation, she said, isn't very large. A lot of their members are older. And they've been without a pastor for some time. But she said she was hopeful that together they could spark renewal. "I'm thinking," she said, "that maybe this could be a project for more than just my church. Several council members (on both sides of the 'fence,' so to speak) are active in their own churches, so that might be an avenue." And another local pastor had married into a powerful town family; she thought that he may be an ally for positive change. "I'm not giving up," she said.

This woman believes that the churches in town—her brothers and sisters in Christ—can be a part of making something new happen. She believes that, through them, God can bring healing and reconciliation. She believes in the possibility of transformation. And she seems ready to let that power be at work in and through her for the sake of her community.

The Kingdom Is among Us!

I don't know if your congregation is full of people willing to take these kinds of hope-filled risks for the sake of your community and our world, but it ought to be.

In mainstream congregations across the globe, in every known language, we pray these words every single Sunday morning: "Our Father, who art in heaven, hallowed be thy name, thy kingdom come, thy will be done, on earth as it is in heaven." These words begin what we call the "Lord's Prayer," because Jesus told us to use them (Matt. 6:9-13; Luke 11:2-4). In other words, Jesus himself told us to pray for his kingdom to come—on earth.

Now, obviously, this kingdom Jesus is talking about isn't a "place." It is, rather, a new reality. It is a transformed world. He tells us about it through his parables, and he showed us what it looked like throughout his life. Jesus says that in this new world even the smallest good deeds make an enormous difference (Luke 13:18-21); the tables are turned on the powerful, and the marginalized and forgotten are honored and treated with respect (14:15-24); and there are no persons so lost that God can't find them (15:3-10). In this new reality, Jesus shows us, there is a place for the littlest ones among us (18:15-17); God works through those whose names we don't even know to change the world (10:1-20); and there is more than enough food to go around when we open up our picnic baskets to share what we have with each other (9:10-17). This is the "kingdom" Jesus tells us to pray for. And don't think for a second that Jesus would instruct us to pray for something that is not possible.

In fact, from Jesus' perspective, we can expect the coming of God's kingdom with apparently no less confidence than we can expect to receive "our daily bread." Using Jesus' words, we pray for these two things in almost the same breath. Furthermore, we can expect to receive them both every single day.

The kingdom of God is not something that exists just in some far-off future. Jesus put that idea to rest when he told the Pharisees not to look for signs of the kingdom. "It is not coming with things that can be observed," he said, "nor will they say, 'Look, here it is!' or 'There it is!' For, in fact, the kingdom of God is among you" (Luke 17:20-21). The kingdom of God, Jesus said, is right here. It is right now. It comes *to* us, everyday. And it comes *through* us to others. We should be no more and no less surprised by it than we are when our toast pops up in the morning.

Living in this new reality, eyes wide open to the miracles that God is working in and through us every day, the people you sit and sing next to on Sunday morning should be full of hope and courage because they believe things really can be different. They should expect to experience God's transformational power at work in and through them, every single day.

Expectant Living

The above description is how you would expect things to be for those of us who pray in Jesus' words every Sunday morning. And in the congregations we visited during our research project, that is what we found.

Again and again we heard stories from the people we interviewed about how God's miraculous power had transformed their lives. At Alleluia, one lay member told us, "The Holy Spirit is at work in this building. There is no other way to put it. It's like a beacon." Similarly, another lay member in that congregation told us that, at Alleluia, people believe "the Holy Spirit is at work in your life and it changes you and you like that change in your life. And you want to share that. [It's] not just 'I stand, I sit, I go through the motions, I go home.'" At Alleluia, he said, something "changes you on the inside, and it's obvious."

Even more dramatically, we heard stories from people about miracles they had seen God work in their lives. One Blessed to Be a Blessing member told us that he had been a nonbeliever his whole life. Two years ago, he said, he was in the hospital with a failing heart. He weighed 370 pounds. Today, since getting involved in this congregation, he is a new man. His weight is down, and both his blood pressure and cholesterol are normal. He is not taking any medication anymore. He told us that, at first, his family thought the congregation had "brainwashed" him. But then, he said, his mother got cancer. Believing in God's transformational power, he described laying his hands on his mother in prayer. Today she is cancer-free. Not long ago, there were no believers in his family, he said. Now his parents are both members of Blessed to Be a Blessing.

We heard similar stories over and over from the people we interviewed in these congregations. From the senior pastors to the newest members, we were told about the miracles—small and large—that God is doing and has done in the lives of ordinary people. We experienced a palpable sense of expectation that God would show up and make new things happen in people's lives. Transformation, in other words, isn't something that happens once in a while in these congregations. It is an expected part of the Christian experience there.

One of the pastoral staff members at Changed Lives, for example, explained that their message is that if you know Jesus, "you will want to tell your neighbor about it . . . and the by-product of that is that God might heal your marriage. God might heal your relationship with your children. God might heal you from your pornography addiction." She said, "God really wants to transform lives in addition to saving them." Likewise, one of the pastors at Blessed to Be a Blessing described how, early on in the ministry there, staff and leaders of the congregation came to believe that "God could heal people today." They say they saw it happen. Now "there's a sense of expectation around here," he told us, "that God can do anything." All of the leaders we interviewed in these congregations were very quick to say that "healing comes in all kinds of ways." And this particular leader explained that they choose to "pray for everyone and see some people healed, instead of praying for no one and seeing no one healed."

Now my guess is that talking about "miracles" and "healing" and "transformation" makes some of us in mainstream churches just a little nervous. There are a lot of different reasons for that. And some of them are good reasons, especially when the expected "transformation" looks too much like the kind of individualistic, moralistic, straitjacket that can squeeze the life—and love—right out of you. I'm talking here about the idea some Christians have that a little Jesus will "straighten" you right up. And there was just enough of this kind of edge in some of the interviews I conducted to make me a teeny bit nervous about all this transformation talk too.

But, as if sensing my concern, the senior pastor at Blessed to Be a Blessing was very clear that individual transformation is connected to service in the world. He insisted that because of his reading of the biblical story, the change he expects to see in a person's life is not con-fined to the suffocating and ultimately self-serving realm of personal morality. Rather, he teaches that transformation is ultimately about loving and serving one's neighbor. In fact, he was able to diagram the process for us. Based on what he believes is a "biblical foundation," he described four "practices" of the congregation. The first is *invitation*: Blessed to Be a Blessing welcomes people to Jesus Christ. The second is *life change*: the invitation leads to a changed life. The third is called *new community*: because of their life change, people want to experi-ence this new life in a community. And the fourth is called *community impact*: a changed life serves its purpose in "ministry, mission, and the marketplace." These practices are taught and reinforced at Blessed to Be a Blessing as members are invited to "tell changed life stories" as a part of each worship service.

Nervous or not, we couldn't help but be impressed as the people we interviewed gave compelling testimony to the transformational power of God in their lives and the lives of their loved ones. They are convinced that God is at work in and through them bringing healing and wholeness.

They believe in miracles.

What's New?

I am convinced that belief in the transformational power of God is one of the reasons the congregations we studied are thriving. People in these congregations are encouraged, in teaching and preaching, to anticipate that something will *happen* as a result of their encounter with Jesus Christ. And, when something does happen, those stories are shared and celebrated. Transformation is expected.

This is not my experience in most mainstream congregations. In fact, too often we suffer from painfully low expectations, even about the simplest things. For example, recently, as I was doing an "asset mapping" exercise with a large group of congregational leadership teams, one team just sat there not participating, looking glum. When I asked them what was going on, they explained that they had done the first part of the exercise. They had listed all of the "assets" they had—talents, friends, community connections, financial resources, passions, facilities, skills, and other resources they could use to do creative ministry in and for the sake of their communities—but they couldn't figure out what those things added up to. In other words, they couldn't decide what to *do* together with all the gifts God had given them.

"Why is this so hard?" I asked, looking at the impressive list of resources spread out before them.

"Because we're so burned out with everything we've been doing," one of them admitted, "that we can't possibly imagine anything new."

With those five sad words, this discouraged bunch unknowingly diagnosed the condition that makes reclaiming the "E" word so elusive for so many mainstream Christians: *We can't imagine anything new.*

When Jesus sent his disciples out on their first real, solo adventure, he told them "to proclaim the kingdom of God and to heal" (Luke 9:2). In other words, he said: "Go tell everybody that because of me, anything is possible! Tell them that God is on the loose and at work in the world! Tell them that a new reality has begun! And live your life as if you believe this is true."

What's *new* is at the very center of the evangelical message we have been given to share with the world. For example, I believe that today our job is to tell everybody who will listen that because of Jesus, there are no more "lines" between people of different races, that we all are children of the same heavenly Parent. It's our job to tell people that God has blessed the human family with plenty of resources to go around and that we are responsible for making sure all people have what they need. It is our job to tell people that the true measure of our lives isn't how much power or wealth we have but, rather, that we are loved unconditionally by the one who created us all, and that we are free, therefore, to serve one another in love. And it is our job to live our lives as if we believe all of this is true.

But saying and doing these things is dependent on our ability to *imagine something new.*

Built for Transformation

We may be helped by remembering that, in a way, transformation is built into our theological DNA. This is true for every mainline Christian. For Lutherans, our theological genetic code is set within the articles of the Augsburg Confession, a document that emerged out of the sixteenth-century Reformation. The first four articles describe the triune God, who has lovingly created all things; the rebellion of humanity; and the saving act of Jesus Christ, through whom humanity is justified and reconciled to God, by grace, through faith. In Article 5 of the Augsburg Confession, we are told that this faith is a gift of the Holy Spirit, who comes to us when we hear the gospel (i.e., the good news about Jesus). And Article 6 is called "Concerning the New Obedience." Here we are taught that the result of faith is a changed life that produces "good fruits." Transformation, in other words, is at the very core of our theological identity. We have been built for change.

Consider that two thousand years ago those first disciples' lives were forever changed by Jesus' simple—and simply miraculous—invitation "Come follow me." The fact is, when you are met by Jesus, something always happens. More specifically, something happens to you, and something happens through you for the sake of others.

One of the exercises I do with groups of congregational leaders to help them understand how this works involves crayons, glue sticks, and newspapers. First, I invite them in groups of four or five to draw Jesus "at the crossroads" (Matt. 4:12-17). Then I ask them to make a collage using words, phrases, and pictures they cut out of their local newspaper to describe what Jesus is up to—and what Jesus wants to be up to—at the crossroads. In other words, I say, describe the good stuff you see happening out there—the places where healing, reconciliation, forgiveness, and freedom are happening. Then describe the bad stuff—the violence, brokenness, and pain—the things you know Jesus wants to change. Usually, after a few seconds of eye rolling (when was the last time *you* made a collage?), people really get into the assignment. They converse about what they see happening "at the cross-roads" in their communities, and they work together to produce something they are proud to share with the other groups. And I ask them to do that when they are ready. Then I challenge them to do one more thing.

"Look at the headlines you've assembled, to describe what Jesus is up to—and what he wants to be up to—in this community."

They look around the room at the work they and their brothers and sisters have done together.

"Think about this: If we dare to follow Jesus to the crossroads and do what it is we are supposed to do, as people who have been called to participate in God's loving mission to save and reconcile and bless the whole world, what will be different? In other words, what will these headlines say about our community ten years from now?"

Each person is given a chance to write down several "headlines" from God's preferred future. They always vary somewhat, depending on the context, but invariably the headlines include such things as: "Racism Eliminated in Our Town," "No Child Goes to Bed Hungry," "Crime Rate Drops Dramatically; Prisons Empty."

What is always a little surprising to me is how easy it is for people to imagine something new once they are engaged by the biblical story and given permission to dream. But it shouldn't be surprising. After all, transformation is in our DNA.

Transformational Power

A friend of mine who does a lot of her work with people who live in Appalachia tells me that once upon a time the preachers in mountain churches were "owned" by the mining companies. They preached company approved "pie in the sky in the by and by" sermons, promising people that "one day" things would be better for them. This kept people going in the midst of horrific living situations and deadly work conditions. It kept them quiet.

And it kept them in bondage. It wasn't until people began to demand "ham in the pan"—and believed that it could be theirs today— that things started to change. In other words, my friend says, a "realized eschatology"[1] is necessary for anything new to happen.

Similarly, we have to believe that the kingdom of God really is at hand if, in fact, we are going to be able share the evangelical message that God is doing and has done a new thing. We have to expect transformation today.

When that happens and people really believe that God is on the loose and at work in our world, they become ready and willing to put themselves on the line—to give away their money and their time; to speak truth to power; to stand out in the crowd; to use their reputations, their influence, their hands, and their voices; to unleash their creativity with joyful abandon; and to risk everything to make a difference in their community and in our world because they know without a doubt that God can be trusted to make things right. They are willing, even, to step into the middle of a divided town to remind everyone that all the healing and reconciliation and peace that we could ever want or need has already been given to the human family by the one who created us.

They are able to share the good news. And they are able to live as if they know it is true.

Wrestling with the Word

1. In Acts 17:16-34, we find the apostle Paul in Athens where he is waiting for some friends. While he is there, in the most unlikely place, he finds evidence that God is on the loose and at work in people's lives. He discovers that his job is simply to "name" what God has already been doing. Read that story now. Where does Paul find evidence that "the kingdom" has already come? What does he do about that? What does he say? What happens?

2. Skim through the biblical story and think about how many characters have their names changed after an encounter with the living God. Abram becomes Abraham. Sarai becomes Sarah. Saul becomes Paul. Can you think of others? What do you think is going on here? What other evidence can you find in the biblical story that meeting God results in transformation?

Thinking Things Through

1. How has your life been changed by your experience of God's love, the healing touch of Jesus Christ, and/or the power of the Holy Spirit?

2. If you really lived as if "the kingdom" is coming and has already come, what would you do differently? How would you be different?

3. Who needs to hear that God can—and has—made all things new? What are you going to tell them? When?

Talking It Over

Dear God, your kingdom is coming—and it has come! Help us see it in our everyday lives. Give us courage to announce it. And teach us to live as if it is true. In Jesus' name, amen.

A Final Word

Looking for a good Bible study to help spark a little evangelical zeal in your sleepy mainstream faith community? Invite people to open up Mark 4:35—5:20 with you. Ask them to read this story together and spend time talking about what they hear God saying to them through it. Encourage them not to talk about what "Mark" is saying or what they "think" this story is about or what this story "means." We spend altogether too much time in the church today arguing about what "the Bible" is saying. Invite people to listen for what *God* is saying to them through this biblical story. It's a good one.

Recently I spent the day in this text with a group of mainline church leaders who had asked me to come facilitate a visioning retreat for them. Most of them had never read the "two" stories in this passage—Jesus calming the storm and his encounter with the Gerasene demoniac—as one. But when you do that, you can't help but notice that this is, in fact, a great story about God's mission in the world and our call to participate in it.[1] In other words, this is a story for those of us who are committed to reclaiming the "E" word.

Jesus tells his disciples to get in a boat with him because, he says, he's going over "to the other side" of the lake. On their way over, a big storm kicks up. Jesus is asleep in the boat and the disciples wake him up. Big, tough guys that they are, they are terrified. Jesus calms the storm and chastises the disciples. "What are you so afraid of?" When they arrive on the other side of the lake, the answer to that question becomes clear. They get out of the boat and are met by a man who says his name is Legion because he has so many demons inside of him. After some negotiating, Jesus casts out the demons and tells the man to go home to his family. A lot of the people who see this happen are scared and ask Jesus to leave. He does. But the man, who by now must have a new name, tells everyone in town what Jesus has done, and they are all amazed.

Here are a couple of other things that we heard God saying to us through this story that day:

Dare to Go to "The Other Side"

We realized that "the other side" is exactly the place Jesus wants to take us. It seemed obvious, as we read these "two" stories together, that what the disciples were really afraid of as they sailed across the sea that night couldn't possibly have been the storm. I mean, they were fishermen, right? They had weathered hundreds of storms at sea.

No, what got them shaking in their waders was the fact that Jesus was taking them over "to the other side." There were scary people over there, unclean people, people who were "different," who didn't believe—or live—the "right" way. The disciples were afraid of encountering the unknown, and they had already decided that it would be bad.

Jesus saw things differently. In fact, in some ways, his whole ministry was about crossing the kinds of boundaries we are afraid or unwilling to cross. That is the kind of ministry he calls us to today.

We'll need more than courage as we go, though. As we step into the presence of those who are different from us—who come from different ethnic, generational, cultural, and even religious backgrounds—we can go boldly, carrying the good news of Jesus Christ. But we must also go in a spirit of deep humility, knowing that the Spirit of God has gone before us and has been at work in and through the lives of the people we encounter.

If you have read the story, you know that the first thing the strange, scary man with all the demons on the other side of the lake did when he saw Jesus was to bow down before him. This guy recognized Jesus as the "Son of the Most High God" before most of his own disciples did!

We will be surprised, if we allow ourselves to be, by the things we will learn from those who are different from us. We will be startled by the way in which they help us understand ourselves, our culture, our scriptures, and even our God better than we ever did before. We will be changed by them in ways that we cannot even begin to imagine now.

As we follow Jesus over to "the other side," with good news to share, we should go in a spirit of bold humility. And, by all means, we should go.[2]

Participate in God's Mirror

Unlike a lot of the rhetoric that is often used by "Evangelical" (here I'm using the term in the way it usually is used today) Christians about needing to "take Jesus" to the lost, in this story the disciples don't take Jesus anywhere. Jesus takes them! Jesus basically says, "Look, I'm going over there. Are you coming or not?"

Few mainline Christians have ever been comfortable with that "saving the lost" language, anyway. It's not that this isn't "biblical" language. It is, of course. But so is language that encourages slaves to obey their masters. The point is that we need to filter our language choices through a theological lens, even when that language has come from the Bible. And, as a Lutheran, my theological lens tells me that such a neat division of the population isn't possible. As a Christian, I am *simul justus et peccator*. That's a fancy Latin phrase that theologians use to talk about the way we are simultaneously justified through Christ and hopeless sinners. We are, in other words, at the same time both "saved" and "lost." There is no way we can start drawing "lines" between us and them; any lines we draw would have to go right down the middle of each one of us. And, make no mistake, using language like "the lost" is as good as drawing a big, fat line.

Reclaiming the "E" word will require, for those of us in the mainline, some serious theological reflection. What exactly are we doing when we "evangelize," anyway? What precisely does it mean to be called into participation in God's mission? Why do you feel compelled to share the good news about what God is up to? What do you think will happen in the world and in the lives of people if you share it? What is God's dream for us and for creation? What does it mean for us to participate in God's mission to make that dream come true? And how are your answers to these questions consistent with what you believe to be true about God, Jesus, the world, heaven, hell, your neighbor, yourself?

Although I can't answer all of those questions for you, it does seem clear to me that our job as Christians is, in some ways, as simple as this: to go with Jesus wherever he goes and to participate in whatever God is doing. It is the basic evangelical task—in other words, to be on the lookout for what God is doing and to be willing to name what we see for people. Jesus said it this way: "The kingdom of heaven is among you!" We might say it like this: "Hey, that looks like God at work!"

My suggestion is that you practice sharing this message on the people who are closest to you, the ones who won't scare easily. Try it on your partner or your kids at dinner one night. Be on the lookout for God at work in and through them during the day, and tell them about it. See what happens in them, in you, and in your family. And, once you get the hang of it, try it out on your coworkers and schoolmates. Try it out on strangers you meet.

It is not your job to "save" these people. But it is your job to tell them what you see and to invite them to see it too.

Expect Jesus to Work Miracles

Mainline Christians have been—and are—in the middle of a storm, all right. Some observers are predicting that, unless something changes *fast*, we will "turn out the lights" on our denominations in this generation.

Now, I'm not saying there aren't problems. In fact, I sometimes am so frustrated by our preoccupations with things that distract us from doing our job that I could scream. For example, is sex the most important thing we have to talk about? Because we talk about it an awful lot. From where I'm standing, it often seems like we are determined to drown out here, lost at sea.

But through this story, I am hearing God say to those of us in mainstream churches, "Whoa. Calm down. Have you no faith?"

The world desperately needs the good news—the really good news—that we have to share. But we aren't going to be able to share it if we are shaking in our waders, huddled in the bottom of the boat, crying like little babies.

Jesus is headed on over to the other side. If even the wind and the sea obey him, what are we waiting for?

Acknowledgments

I am indebted to Ken Inskeep and his team at the Department for Research and Evaluation of the Evangelical Lutheran Church in America. Working alongside them for the research portion of this project was a privilege, and although I take full responsibility for the analysis and interpretation of the data as it has been presented here, they were invaluable conversation partners during the entire process. Plus, they're fun to hang out with. Thanks, too, to Karin Craven for her assistance at a key point during this project.

To the congregational leaders who allowed us to do a "deep dive" into their ministries, observing them, interviewing them and their members, and drawing conclusions about them as a part of this research project: We all are indebted to you. Although the way you and I understand and practice our faith may differ in some ways, I have profound respect for you and the work you are doing. Thank you for giving us the opportunity to learn from you for the sake of God's mission in the world.

It's also probably time for me to thank Dave Daubert, who is on the ELCA churchwide staff working in the area of congregational renewal. Working with Dave in a variety of ways over the years has been the greatest education of my life. I am different because of you, Dave. One just doesn't find colleagues—or friends—like you very often, and I'm thankful for you.

I am thankful, too, for all those people across the church who let me into their congregations, their judicatory offices, their denominational units, and their lives so I could "mess" with things. Together we do all kinds of good work: revisioning, restructuring, realigning, renewing, retooling. But I learn as much and probably more from you than you do from me. Plus, you tell me great stories! Thanks for letting me use them.

To my kids: Thanks for filling my life with laughter. Your hopeful spirits and unconditional love, through all of the wacky changes we've been through together over the past several years, have truly been an evangelical witness to me. Through you, I have heard the really good news, and it has been healing for my soul.

Finally, a word to Tana. Your fingerprints are all over my work. They have been for almost as long as I can remember. In fact, I think it is not an exaggeration to say that every great idea I've ever had was hatched first in your imagination. I am more thankful than I can say that you are my partner in ministry, in life, and in every imaginable sense of that word.

Notes

All websites accessed October 26, 2007.

Chapter 1

1. Patrick Allitt, who teaches history at Emory University, calls the period from 1976 to 1990 "Evangelicals and Politics." For more information about this era in American church history, see Allitt's book *Religion in America Since 1945: A History* (New York: Columbia University Press, 2003).

2. Cathy Lynn Grossman, "Can the 'E Word' be Saved?" *USA Today*, January 23, 2007.

3. Ibid., 6D.

4. Cathy Lynn Grossman, "View of God Can Reveal Your Values and Politics," *USA Today*, September 12, 2006.

5. John Buckeridge, "The E Word," *Christianity*, May 2006.

6. Allitt, *Religion in America Since 1945*, 152.

7. Church historians and sociologists credit Robert Wuthnow, author of *The Restructuring of American Religion* (Princeton, N.J.: Princeton University Press, 1988), with recognizing this shift.

8. Kelly A. Fryer, "Act Boldly for Mission: Session 1," *Lutheran Woman Today*, June 2007.

9. For seventy-five years The National Council of Churches has published a Yearbook of American and Canadian Churches. For more information visit www.ncccusa.org/.

10. This is, in fact, the argument made compellingly by Robert Bacher and Kenneth Inskeep in *Chasing Down a Rumor: The Death of Mainline Denominations* (Minneapolis: Augsburg Fortress, 2005), 84.

11. See Bacher and Inskeep, *Chasing Down a Rumor*, 13. The authors report this data to support a similar conclusion.

12. Allitt, *Religion in America Since 1945*, 259–60.

13. Mark Kelley in a piece called "Seven—In God's Army," which originally aired on December 19, 2006, on *The National*, a CBCNews program, www.cbc.ca/national/archive/category.html?seven_mark_kelley.

14. Bacher and Inskeep, *Chasing Down a Rumor*, 84.

Chapter 2

1. Mother Teresa's letters have been published in a book titled *Mother Teresa: Come Be My Light*, ed. Brian Kolodiejchuk (New York: Doubleday, 2007). David Van Biema tells the story in "Her Agony," *Time*, September 3, 2007.

2. Philipp Jakob Spener, "Pia Desideria (1675)," in *Pietists: Selected Writings*, ed. Peter Erb (New York: Paulist, 1983).

3. Richard Bliese and Craig Van Gelder, eds., *The Evangelizing Church: A Lutheran Contribution* (Minneapolis: Augsburg Fortress, 2005), 39.

4. Bliese, Van Gelder, and the team of authors they worked with on *The Evangelizing Church* argue that "Word, Sacrament, and Christian community" is the richest and most confessionally accurate way of describing in theological "shorthand" the means by which Christ promises to come to us.

5. This is also the "big idea" behind my first book in the reclaiming series, *Reclaiming the "L" Word: Renewing the Church from Its Lutheran Core* (Minneapolis: Augsburg Fortress, 2003).

6. See Bliese and Van Gelder, *The Evangelizing Church*. This idea may be "Lutheranism's unique contribution to missiology in our context: a definition of evangelizing that ties the word of the cross not to ministry methods, church growth, Christian disciplines, liturgical forms, social status, contextual dynamics, or musical style, but simply to the concrete coming of Jesus in Word, Sacrament, and Christian community" (p. 40). But it's not an automatic. The fact is, these means of grace are being held captive. This book is, in some ways, a call to freedom . . . so that Word, Sacrament, and Community become, once again, the life-giving means of grace they are intended to be.

7. The names of individuals and any details about them that would reveal their true identities have been changed.

Chapter 3

1. See also *Lutheran Women Today*, June 2007, for a similar telling of this story.

2. Emily Nunn, "The Street Preacher," *Chicago Tribune,* July 30, 2004.

3. Fred Gaiser is a respected Old Testament scholar who teaches at Luther Seminary in St. Paul, Minnesota. This is from a helpful essay he wrote titled "The Heresy of Infallibility," *Word and World*, Fall 2006. It is available on-line at www.luthersem.edu/word&world/EditorialFall2006.asp.

4. Martin Luther, *Christian Liberty* (Philadelphia: Fortress Press, 1957), 8.

5. These three questions meant to help people learn to listen for God's living voice through biblical stories are at the heart of an eight-unit series called *No Experience Necessary Bible Study* (Minneapolis: Augsburg Fortress, 2005, 2006, and 2007).

Chapter 4

1. This story is also used as the basis for a Bible study I wrote that was published in the *2007–2008 Christian Education Planning Guide*, ELCA, 2007.

2. See Kelly A. Fryer, *No Experience Necessary: Everybody's Welcome* (Minneapolis: Augsburg Fortress, 2005). This idea is explored in chapter three.

3. Martin Luther, *Christian Liberty* (Philadelphia: Fortress Press, 1957), 29.

4. This is, in a sense, correcting the single, downward arrow that appears in my book *Reclaiming the "L" Word: Renewing the Church from Its Lutheran Core* (Minneapolis: Augsburg Fortress, 2001). That arrow only tells half the story. The whole story is that we are saved by grace through faith in Jesus Christ so that we can serve our neighbor. Both arrows are necessary to understand what it means to be "a Christian who happens to be a Lutheran."

5. J. C. Hoekendijk, *The Church Inside Out* (Philadelphia: Westminster, 1964), 24.

6. Ibid., 15.

7. For example, the theologian Hoekendijk found himself on the opposite side of the table from (Lesslie Newbigin) is widely credited with sparking the contemporary missiological conversation, and his name is revered across denominational lines. Happily, at least one other missiologist on the scene today is attempting to resurrect and build on Hoekendijk's work. See Steve Bevans, "God Inside Out: Notes toward a Missionary Theology of the Holy Spirit," www.sedos.org/english/Bevans.html.

8. Hoekendijk, *The Church Inside Out*, 70.

Chapter 5

1. Martin Luther, "The German Mass and Order of Service," Luther's Works, vol. 53 (Philadelphia: Fortress Press, 1957), 61.

2. Ibid.

3. Ibid., 62.

4. Ibid., 63.

5. Ibid.

6. Ibid.

7. Brian Hindo, "At 3M: A Struggle between Efficiency and Creativity," Business Week, June 11, 2007.(www.businessweek.com/magazine/content/07_24/b4038406. htm?chan=top+news_top+news+index_best+of+bw)

Chapter 6

1. Eschatology is a theological term that traditionally means a study of the "end times," including the destiny of humanity and the final events in the history of the world. A "realized eschatology" focuses, instead, on the new reality that Jesus has already brought and is bringing into the world. Thanks to Helen Harms for this powerful illustration.

A Final Word

1. Thanks to Rick Bliese (now president of Luther Seminary) for sharing this insight with me and other students in the graduate seminar he taught many years ago at the Lutheran School of Theology at Chicago.

2. The concept of humble boldness was taught—and lived—by the twentieth-century missiologist and missionary Lesslie Newbigin.

For Further Reading

Robert Bacher and Ken Inskeep. *Chasing Down a Rumor: The Death of Mainline Congregations.* Minneapolis: Augsburg, 2005.

Richard H. Bliese and Craig Van Gelder, eds. *The Evangelizing Church: A Lutheran Contribution.* Minneapolis: Augsburg Fortress, 2005.

John Bowen. *Evangelism for Normal People: Good News for Those Looking for a Fresh Approach.* Minneapolis: Augsburg Fortress, 2002.

Dave Daubert. *Living Lutheran: Renewing Your Congregation.* Minneapolis: Augsburg Fortress, 2007.

Kelly A. Fryer. *Reclaiming the "C" Word: Daring to Be Church Again.* Minneapolis: Augsburg Fortress, 2006.

Kelly A. Fryer. *A Story Worth Sharing: Engaging Evangelism.* Minneapolis: Augsburg Fortress, 2002

Craig Van Gelder. *The Ministry of the Missional Church: A Community Led by the Spirit.* Grand Rapids: Baker, 2007.

Craig Van Gelder. *The Missional Church in Context: Helping Congregations Develop Contextual Ministry.* Grand Rapids: Eerdmans, 2007.

Darrell L. Guder, *The Continuing Conversion of the Church.* Grand Rapids: Eerdmans, 2000.

Alan Roxburgh and Fred Romanuk. *The Missional Leader: Equipping Your Church to Reach a Changing World.* San Francisco: Jossey-Bass, 2006.

Jim Wallis. *God's Politics: Why the Right Gets It Wrong and the Left Doesn't Get It.* New York: HarperCollins, 2005.